Saucepans on our Heads

Ron Burchell

ELSP

Published in 2013 by
ELSP
11 Regents Place
Bradford on Avon
Wiltshire BA15 1ED

Origination by Ex Libris Press
www.ex-librisbooks.co.uk

Printed by CPI Group (UK) Ltd,
Croydon, CR0 4YY

ISBN 978-1-906641-52-8

All enquiries and correspondence regarding this book should be sent to the author at 35 Crombey Street, Swindon, SN1 5QL

Cover picture of Swindon courtesy
of Swindon Libraries

Ackowledgements: Bruce Parkinson
and Sundar Sambandam,
for technical support

CONTENTS

The author's sister, mother and father

Introduction

Reference is often made to the dark days of World War 2. They were days of danger and hardship and for many people great sadness, but there was also a good deal of humour and a wonderful community spirit, the like of which has rarely been seen since.

For the youngsters of the time, the days did not seem to be so dark and dismal for they appeared to be oblivious to the dangers and hardships and treated the experience as an exciting adventure.

I was one of those youngsters, a young lad in a not too well off family of four, and living in a very ordinary house in a typical provincial town

There are many schoolboys who lived in cities that were heavily blitzed and could tell of more horrendous experiences than I, but the memories I have recalled here will give an insight to those who have wondered what it was like to live during those times.

Auntie Lizzie, father and mother at Weston-Super-Mare during the war

The Beginning

I was nine years-old when the war began. I had a sister who was seven years older than me, and our parents were then in their early fifties. We seemed to be the typical happy family of the times. Also regarded as one of the family was the cat. We lived in a three bedroomed terraced house, quite near to the town centre. My school and my sister's place of work were quite close by, which enabled us to have our midday meals at home. Father was not so lucky as he worked on the railway and was not always able to have his meals with us. He began working in railway sidings, coupling wagons together to form a goods train. He then progressed to become a guard on a goods train, and then took on the position of a guard on a passenger train.

In our row of modest houses everyone knew each other and there was a good community spirit, which proved to be an important factor in maintaining morale during times of danger and stress.

At the end of our row of houses lived a retired major. But how a retired major had come to settle here was not clear. Yet he was very sociable, and frequently exchanged morning greetings with father, as they strolled down the garden following their morning wash and brandishing their hand towels. His neighbour was the mother of the house, and she was a worldly lady with blond hair and was the talk of the neighbourhood. Conversations held over the garden walls seemed to be a pleasant part of life, and many titbits of scandal were no doubt exchanged.

All houses in our row had three bedrooms, two rooms downstairs and a kitchen. The toilet was located outside and was certainly no place to take a newspaper to read during the winter months.

Most people kept pets. There was June's noisy and aggressive dog called Spot which was rather a hazard next door, and there was also their wandering tortoise which nibbled at appetising things in the garden when it was not hibernating. Clucking hens and chickens further up the road added to the surrounding sounds of the neighbourhood.

Times might well have been harrowing, but life was never dull, not in our street it wasn't.

Quite a lot of children lived in the area, and our little gang consisted of several lads, and one or two girls, but the girls were certainly not allowed to stay out after dark. They also wisely opted out of the more boisterous activities.

Not every day was boisterous, for Sunday was the day I had to go to church. Our church was known as Anglo-Catholic where candles, vestments and incense were integral parts of the worship. The singing was led by a large choir of boys and men. Fortunately I was never asked to sing in the choir, as singing was not recognised as one of my talents. At this I was quite pleased because choir practice was held on two nights of the week, and was something I would not have looked forward to. Only one other member of the gang was, like me, required to attend church but only, it seemed, on festival occasions such as Easter or Christmas.

It was on those festive occasion that it was often decided to light a fire in the front room. I always enjoyed those occasions, not least because the front room was where the most comfortable furniture was arranged. A fire in the front room may have been more frequent had it not been for the tedious procedure of igniting the paper and wood which had been carefully arranged, and keeping a steady supply of coal available to keep the fire burning. There was also the unenviable task of clearing the ashes from the grate the following morning.

The fact that we were able to enjoy the comforts of a coal fire was due to a strong and dedicated number of workers. First, there was the coal man. I always watched in awe as he made his way down the garden path, carrying, seemingly without effort, a one hundredweight sack of coal on his back, and then deliver the contents into our coal bunker with a thunderous roar and amidst a cloud of dust.

A daunting task also fell to the dustmen whose job it was to empty the dustbins, full of residual ashes and all manner of household waste. They made light work of hoisting the bins on to their shoulders, and made their way to deposit the contents into a dustcart. It was due to the dedication of these workers that we thankfully maintained the coal fire which was the focal point of the house. It was the place where father and mother tended to doze off. It was the place where we gathered to hear the news bulletins on the wireless. But most of all, it was the place where, at the end of the day, the warmth and comforting glow of the embers made the prospect of retiring to a cold bedroom an extremely unattractive option. Most families had their set routines. Rose and her young daughter next door always went to the pictures on a Monday. It mattered not what film was being shown at the cinema, the Monday visit was an established routine.

My father and mother were not too interested in going to the cinema. Mother preferred reading a good book and father was happy listening to the wireless. Friday evening was one of the highlights of the week, for that was the time we went with Rose and June for a stroll round the shops. On a Friday and a Saturday evening the shops remained open until eight o'clock. We lived only five minutes walk away from the shops, which we found to be an advantage in many ways.

One of the shops I found to be most exciting was the shop which sold gramophone records, and where people gathered to watch and admire the radiogram. This electrically powered innovation was a huge improvement on the wind-up gramophone which had a place in my aunt's household.

It was a Friday tradition to visit Woolworth's, where nothing was on sale priced at more than sixpence. This was a store which was extremely popular, and where expertise was needed to attract the attention of the salesgirl behind the counter. They had the unenviable job of taking the money, wrapping the purchase and calculating the change. If mother required to make a purchase, her being quite small was a disadvantage, but she was a battler.

I was always fascinated by the system relating to the payment for items purchased at the Co-op. The money, together with the bill, was placed in a small container. The lid was closed and the container was attached to an overhead track and despatched to the cashier by what appeared to be a catapult mechanism. After a short wait, the container was returned with the change and the receipt. I spent happy times watching the containers travel to and fro before being dragged away.

We always enjoyed our evening trip to the shops which were a hive of activity and brilliantly illuminated. Nearly every shop had a colourful neon-lit sign and advertising signs, some of which flashed on and off, contributing to the spectacle. Cinemas and theatres were also brilliantly illuminated so that the view down the entire length of the street was reminiscent of the pictures I had seen of New York's Broadway. Unfortunately the scene was soon to become a distant memory. Most people were aware of the increasing military threat from Germany, but we were led to believe that a state of war would not be the outcome. While some politicians endorsed this view, I don't think it was a view held with confidence in our household.

We had a good modern wireless in our house, and I enjoyed tuning in to the enormous number of radio stations that could be received. It was during those moments that I was able to pick up, from a German station, the aggressive and ranting voice of Hitler as he addressed numerous rallies in German cities. The supporting chants and cheers from the assembled masses seemed to endorse his fearsome rhetoric and indicated the possibility of troublesome times ahead.

This became more likely as the massive build up of arms and threat of an invasion of Poland caused our political leaders to be of the opinion that something should be done.

In due course Prime Minister Neville Chamberlain flew to Germany to meet Hitler. He returned rather triumphantly and stepped from the plane waving a piece of paper to the waiting crowd, which he claimed had been signed by the German chancellor and would guarantee peace. The complete fallacy of that belief became clear, when shortly afterwards German troops advanced into Poland. A still confident Chamberlain demanded of Hitler a complete withdrawal of German forces and gave an ultimatum that unless he was informed by a given time that such a withdrawal was taking place, then a state of war would exist between the two countries. We all gathered round the wireless when the time came to hear the prime minister address the nation.

I don't think that our gang was particularly concerned whatever the outcome, as we were quite oblivious to the horrors and hardships of war, and I was not at all surprised to find that most of us thought that it could be an exciting adventure. As the family gathered round the wireless in complete silence, I was aware for the first time of a mounting concern, for it seemed perfectly clear what the outcome would be.

The Prime Minister announced in a sombre voice that no such message regarding the withdrawal of German troops had been received, and therefore a state of war existed between the two countries.

The reaction of mother and father and seemingly all of the neighbours was one of grave foreboding, and I began to be of the opinion that this, after all, was not going to be the adventure we had thought it might be.

Our Town Prepares

The declaration of war had momentarily stunned everybody, but soon the mood and atmosphere changed. Information and advice on how to prepare and what to do made our row of houses a hive of activity.

Much had to be done. Conversations over the garden wall were frequent as neighbour updated neighbour on tasks undertaken and progress made. In order to deny enemy aircraft a clear view of Swindon, action to prevent spillage of light after dark became an urgent task. The problem was solved in a variety of ways. The use of black curtains appeared to be a popular choice, but when demand outstripped supply, other solutions had to be found. My father decided to construct wooden frameworks to fit downstairs windows, and cover with lino, which proved to be effective. Unfortunately, this measure was not applied to the upstairs rooms, so at bedtime we had to undress in the dark.

Measures had to be taken to combat the dangers from flying glass as a result of explosions. There was nothing that could be done to give one hundred percent protection, but it was common procedure to stick strips of paper to the window which went some way to counter the threat.

Preparations continued apace. Sandbags were placed around important buildings for protection, and air raid shelters were constructed in public parks and on other open spaces.

A request was made for volunteers to become air raid wardens whose duty, among others, was to ensure that blackout regulations were strictly adhered to and to respond to emergency situations. They operated from suitably protected sites know as wardens posts, and were ready to give assistance to the public at all times. One of their first duties was to take part in an exercise designed to warn people of a poisonous gas attack. Wardens were required to tour their designated – areas waving and sounding rattles, which was a warning for people to put on their gas masks. The signal to indicate that the danger had passed was given by the ringing of hand bells. It was an exercise which brought most people to their front doors, and some neighbours seemed to find the whole thing quite amusing, but I suspect that everyone hoped that the exercise they were watching would not become a reality, especially as many people, including those in our household, had not at the time received gas masks.

It was sometimes difficult to keep up with the pace as one event after another unfolded.

There was an urgent call up of men who were old enough to join the armed forces. Not all men were required to enlist in the services as many were required to do the essential jobs in industry and transport. My father was judged to be in that category in view of his work on the railway, as it was vitally important to keep transport moving

What some people found difficult to accept was the position of the conscientious objector, who was exempt from call up on the grounds of a refusal to take any action which could result in death or injury.

Preparations continued apace and we were informed by the local authority that evacuees would he billeted where accommodation was available. Thousands of children from the London area were evacuated to towns and villages thought to be less of a target for enemy bombers. We as a family of four did not have the accommodation to house any evacuees, as was the situation with our neighbours on one side. Our neighbours on the other side were a middle-aged couple, and having two rooms unoccupied knew that they would be required to house two or three evacuees.

The couple had no children, and appeared to look forward to the prospect of having a family to care for, albeit on a temporary basis. The day soon arrived, and the sound of noisy and excited chatter brought many people to their front doors, where they were confronted by many children and their billeting officers.

Gladys and Bill were happy to welcome into their home three children: Donald and Joey from East Ham, and Tommy from Poplar. It must have been a very harrowing time for the children to have been separated from their parents, and not knowing when they would see them again.

Gladys at once did her utmost to make them feel at home, and I wondered whether, after they had settled here, they would become members of our gang. This never came to pass, for although they seemed to be happy enough with their new home, they preferred to keep themselves to themselves.

However, one who did arrive sometime later and was housed in the next street took no time at all to consider himself one of the gang. Len, a confident 11 year-old from Poplar, and acting far older than his age, never ceased to amuse us with his stories and recollections. On one occasion he told us rather sadly that having lived in the deprived and crowded east end of London, he had never seen a cow, or even a blade of grass. We were prepared to go along with his not seeing a cow, but pulled his leg endlessly about the apparent absence of grass. However, in a short time he became a likeable and leading member of our happy band.

The advent of the blackout was the first hazardous wartime situation that the public had to face, and the gang's regular evening meetings on the street corner looked to be in jeopardy. To move around after dark had to be done with confidence and great care. A torch was most vital for pedestrians. For the motorist, shades fitted to headlights, which kept light spillage to a minimum, was a necessity.

Worries regarding the gang's meetings after dark proved to be unfounded as a steely determination ensured that the meetings continued.

It took only a short time for our family to become accustomed to the blackout conditions, and evening appointments and engagements carried on much the same as before.

However, the hours of darkness, and the likelihood of enemy air attack during that time, gave rise to the need for another group of volunteers called fire watchers. They were required during the hours of darkness to be on the lookout for fires likely to be started by incendiary bombs. There was no shortage of volunteers for the task, and the organiser compiled a duty roster which was posted in the front window of his house, so that those involved could see when their turn of duty came around. Both sexes were involved, and the gang's comedian was quick to point out that there would, no doubt, be times when fires and bombs would bc the furthest thing from their minds.

There was plenty of information and advice on how to deal with fires. The use of an appliance called a stirrup pump, which was small and easily handled by two people, was regarded as the most effective way for residents in the average household to tackle incendiary bombs.

The basic apparatus consisted of a hand operated suction pump submerged in a bucket of water, which when operated pumped water along a length of hose. One person operated the suction pump, while another directed the water spray towards the incendiary device, but doing so from a precautionary prone position.

Firemen organised and supervised stirrup pump training sessions for residents in our street. These proved to be very popular as residents felt the need to be thoroughly prepared to face fire hazards arising from enemy air attack. The gang were keen to be involved and they also underwent a thorough training. Firemen were also involved in a more substantial fire fighting exercise, which often took place on the banks of a huge lake at the back of our house. Water was pumped from the lake by way of a motorised pump, first through a basket filter, which had been submerged, and then along a length of hose, and was finally ejected with considerable force through a nozzle held and wrestled manfully by two burly firemen.

This was an entertainment not to be missed, as it was not unusual to see one or two firemen receive a good soaking. Great care was taken not to stand too close, or laugh out loud, in case the hose was turned in our direction, as the firemen often threatened.

This method of extracting water was quickly regarded as an important fire fighting facility, and saw the emergence of huge static water tanks erected in strategic places around the town.

Some households had water butts situated adjacent to the back of the house, and were in position to collect water flowing from the roof guttering during heavy rainstorms. Although, in many cases, they were in place some time before the war, they were conveniently to hand should an emergency water supply be needed.

Quite a lot had been achieved by way of preparation and training in a short time, and residents felt confident that, as far as an attack by fire bombs was concerned, they were as prepared as they possibly could be. As far as the lads were concerned, hazards of a different kind were looming. Some of us had left elementary school and begun a five year educational period at secondary school, having passed an exam called the scholarship. What an important land mark that was in a young man's life, and made even more exciting by the change from short to long trousers.

It became clear very quickly that discipline and regimentation were very important to the school. We were required to wear a school uniform, and a satchel was needed in which to carry numerous books. Gas masks, which most children had received by then, also had to be taken to school so that they could be tested for safety and reliability.

Teachers were addressed as Miss or Sir, and misbehaviour earned a detention after school. More serious breaches of discipline resulted in the administering of a cane to the backside. Such hazards were not without humour as some of us stuffed exercise books down the back of our trousers in an effort to deaden the impact. Most pupils, including myself, got away with it. I was neither a classroom rebel or an angel, but I had a strange feeling that I was never going to be a brilliant pupil, or reach the academic heights that my sister had attained during her education at the school seven years before me.

During the early days of the war, there was fear of an enemy attack involving poisonous gas, and it was deemed necessary that the gas masks issued to the pupils were to be tested on a regular basis. This always proved to be a humorous occasion, even though the form mistress tried hard to make it a serious exercise.

'Will you please take your gas masks out of the case and put them in front of you,' said the form mistress. There followed an excitable burst of activity and chatter.

'Have you all done that?'

"Yes miss,' the class replied. Then came the order, 'Gas masks on'.

The mask was held in both hands and positioned under

the chin, which enabled it to be pulled up over the face by way of a rubber strap, which slid over the back of the head to hold the mask in place. There was an eye piece above the large snout-like filter, which afforded adequate vision for the wearer. During this time muffled laughter could be heard as pupils viewed each other and found the situation quite amusing.

'Settle down,' ordered a rather annoyed mistress, but by now everyone was breathing in and out with gusto, and the rebel of the class knew from experience that exhaling vigorously produced a peculiar sound.

'Sounds like somebody farting,' he loudly announced, causing gales of laughter around the class.

'That's quite enough of that,' warned the form mistress as she prepared to test each mask, while making the point that the class comedian was lucky to escape without a detention.

To test the mask, a piece of card was held against the filter as the wearer inhaled. If the card remained in position, the mask was deemed to be in proper working order and offered maximum protection.

All passed the test, and not surprisingly the gas mask check was seen as a pleasant diversion from lessons, and something to look forward to. Another pleasant diversion came during the morning break, when we were provided with our small daily bottle of milk The bottle held one third of a pint and cost one halfpenny. Monday was milk money day when the form mistress collected our money for the five days supply. This routine continued without interruption throughout the days of the war. This was deemed necessary to keep us in good health, and aid our physical development.

Good health and good spirits were much needed at that time, not only for us, but for the whole of the nation, for during the forthcoming months the resolve and fortitude of the British people would be given a very tough test.

The First War-time Christmas

Christmas was soon upon us, and most people were determined to make the first Christmas of the war as enjoyable as possible.

There was much to be done. First, it was mother's job to write the cards, while father wrote what was his annual letter to his sister.

It was worth staying in to listen to the tetchy verbal exchanges, as mother continually consulted an irritated father over the suitability of her chosen cards for particular friends and relatives.

There was also the Christmas shopping to be done, as wartime circumstances had not suspended the practice of giving presents.

I always enjoyed being invited in to the kitchen to help with the making of Christmas puddings. Mother made the puddings in a large bowl, and all the family was invited to stir the mixture and, at the same time, to make a wish. This had apparently been a tradition. Several puddings were made, and some were kept to celebrate birthdays which fell during the first part of the year. Food preparations continued with the making of the Christmas cake, which was kept until nearer the time, when it was then iced, adorned with cake decorations, and topped off with a little father Christmas. It needed skill and ingenuity to scrape together and utilise what in many cases were substitute ingredients, such as dried egg and powdered milk, and mother had the skill to turn out puddings and cakes with mouth-watering effect.

At school it was also felt important to celebrate the festive season. The school was mixed and I discovered with slight trepidation that pupils were expected to attend what was called a Christmas soirée. The boys were encouraged to take a girl to the dance, rather than have a situation where boys and girls gazed at each other across the hall. I knew that it wasn't my cup of tea because dancing was certainly not one of my talents, but looking back I think that I had made a good stab at it.

The autumn term came to a conclusion with the final assembly. Carols and festive songs were sung and enthusiastically conducted by our ebullient headmaster, who always appeared to thoroughly enjoy the occasion. It always surprises me that I can still remember the following verse, which we sang as a round with enthusiasm and gusto:

Without the door let sorrow lie
And if perchance it hap to die
We'll bury it in the Christmas pie
And ever more be merry.

My sister and I were responsible for the Christmas decorations. We decorated the dining room with paper chains, which we had made by sticking together coloured strips of paper, and added balloons dotted around the room. We also arranged decorative paper around the pendant lampshade which made a colourful effect. On Christmas day a fire was lit in the front room, as it was on most festive occasions, and the day began with a visit to church for the morning service. Following that, we were ready to sit round our large dining room table to enjoy Christmas dinner.

It was very rare that father could spend the whole of

Christmas day with us as a result of having to work an early or late turn of duty on the railway, but on the occasion of the first wartime Christmas we ate dinner together.

There was a tendency for the older ones to doze off after dinner, but they woke up in time to hear the King's Christmas message at three o'clock. In his speech he thanked troops who had arrived from across the Empire to fight alongside British forces. He spoke very slowly and paused frequently, as it seemed difficult for him to overcome a speech impediment.

The Pope also made a speech in which he appealed for peace, which was no more than expected, and that brought the formalities of Christmas to a close.

There was then tea time to enjoy, which consisted of fruit and cream or trifle and a lovely slice of the beautifully iced Christmas cake. It was amazing how, after a large dinner, our stomachs had room for tea, but make room we certainly did, and so another Christmas meal was thoroughly enjoyed. It was also gratifying to see the look of satisfaction on mother's face as the cake was singled out for special praise.

Christmas night was the time for playing games, and singing round the piano. My sister was quite good at playing our piano which looked ancient to me even by the standards of the time. The sound produced left quite a lot to be desired, but the loveable old piano, standing in pride of place against the wall, was essential to the overall enjoyment of the occasion.

The last meal of the day was supper, and consisted of cold chicken left over from dinner, which was served with salad and pickles.

Looking back at the end of the day, and considering the meals we had eaten, which had been washed down with glasses of port, it was difficult to realise that there was a war on. We anticipated of course, that times would change, and conditions deteriorate, and so it was satisfying that we had enjoyed, as indeed had most families, the first wartime Christmas.

That season of the year was the time for pantomimes. I was never very interested in seeing these shows. They always seemed to me to be far too long, and I began to fidget, but I was taken to them regardless as it had clearly been a tradition seemingly to be honoured. Some members of the gang liked the shows and often boasted of sitting in the rather expensive seats in the dress circle, whereas we, not being so well off, queued early to get good seats in the upper circle.

Mother could never persuade father to go to the theatre or the cinema. He much preferred to listen to the wireless from the comfort of his armchair. There were many good humorous programmes to listen to at that time. Comedy stars Arthur Askey and Richard Murdoch took parts in a show called 'Band Wagon' in which they were purported to be sharing a flat on the roof of Broadcasting House, and where all manner of comedy situations developed. My favourite show was 'ITMA' which was an abbreviation of 'It's That Man Again', starring the fast-talking comedy actor Tommy Handley. Played before a live audience and read from scripts, Handley's rapport with the audience was continually interrupted by a stream of comedy characters. My favourite was a char lady called Mrs Mop whose catch phrase 'Can I Do You Now Sir?' swept the nation.

Listening to the wireless was probably the most popular entertainment at that time. This may have come about, in part, due to problems relating to the blackout. Although our family coped quite well, and the gang's street corner meetings carried on regardless, there had been a considerable number of accidents involving vehicles, and reports of pedestrians bumping into lamp posts and trees. This led to the painting of white lines around these potential hazards, and also on the pavements at street corners, which helped a great deal for those walking along the streets during the hours of darkness.

Waiting and Wondering

With the rather muted new year celebrations out of the way, there was a period of relative calm and most people wondered why. It was certainly very strange that the air raids, which had been widely anticipated, had not materialised, and there was hope that such fearful predictions were wide of the mark. In fact some evacuees, who had become homesick, decided to return to London.

Gladys next door found herself without most of her temporary family as Donald and Joey returned home, but it was clear to see how pleased she was that Tommy decided to stay.

There continued to be little in the way of enemy action over the country, but appeals and campaigns abounded to keep us on our toes.

There was an urgent appeal for waste paper such as newspapers, magazines, comics and cardboard, which we were asked to store alongside our dustbins to be ready for collection. There was a very good response to this appeal, and large quantities of paper were stored at sites which were called salvage depots. There was one such depot in our vicinity, and an enjoyable craze developed as adventurous lads jumped from height into the mass of waste paper below. It was a pastime enjoyed by many until such time as the watchman told us to clear off.

It seemed as though kids had energy to burn. We played

football in the street, climbed trees, and some inventive lads even concocted their own transport. They joined together two short wooden planks, and made them mobile by attaching four small wheels taken from an old pram, and with a primitive steering mechanism operated by guide ropes, they were able to travel down hills at considerable speed, It was not something that I rushed to do, being more interested in somewhat less risky pastimes. I enjoyed paying visits to the cinema with the lads after school, which in those days was called 'going to the pictures'.

At that time several new films were released. One film entitled 'The Wizard Of Oz' proved to be very popular as did an epic called 'Gone With The Wind' but, knowing that this feature lasted over three hours, it was not on our list of films to see. The picture that the gang most enjoyed seeing was the western 'Stagecoach', which featured the ever popular scenes of running battles with the Indians.

I loved the cinema with the spacious auditorium, and well upholstered seats and the seemingly universal appreciation of the cinema's luxurious environment clearly contributed to its popularity.

The programmes usually consisted of two feature films, a newsreel and sometimes a travelogue. Some cinemas provided musical entertainment during the interval where organs were installed, and quite a few organists became household names as a result of popular broadcasts on the BBC.

Our town had two large cinemas in the town centre, and one small one which was known as the flea pit. Films were given one of three classifications. X indicated a horror film, U classified the film as passed for universal viewing, while an A-certificate indicated that viewing was confined to adults and also for children who were accompanied by adults.

In order for the lads to gain entry to see a film with an

A-classification, unusual steps had to he taken. We took up a position so that we could approach adults making their way to the cinema, and then simply asked them to take us in. Most of them usually agreed and so ticket money was handed over, the tickets purchased and, once inside, we gratefully thanked our impromptu guardians and made our way to our favourite seats.

Programmes carried on uninterrupted during the later stages of the war in spite of frequent air raid warnings, but audiences were always informed of an alert by way of a makeshift slide projected onto the screen. Several stars made their names in films during those times: comedy actor George Formby who never seemed to be without his ukulele. Will Hay, the adventurous but accident prone school master, and the antics of the wonderful Laurel and Hardy ensure that such humour would endure for generations to come. There was also a continuous output from the large American studios in Hollywood, which gave us the westerns and gangster films, and ensured such a marvellous choice of entertainment, that a regular visit to the cinema proved to be a very attractive proposition. In time, the film producers saw the opportunity to make patriotic films, and they certainly had the desired effect, for after seeing the well acclaimed film entitled 'In Which We Serve', which charted the harrowing experience of survivors from a sunken warship, one left the cinema with a feeling of pride.

Cinema visits were momentarily forgotten when I arrived home to find that the long expected rationing of food had been announced. Mother was the custodian of the ration books, and was required to register at the shop of her choice. She registered at the Co-op where she had been a member for many years, and I still remember her Co-op number of 1082.

I always enjoyed tagging along when she set out for a Co-op

visit, and was fascinated to watch the shop assistant patting the butter to the required shapes, while at the same time I appreciated the wonderful aroma of the coffee. The whole rationing exercise was confidently dealt with by mother, who purchased rationed food items in exchange for a set number of coupons taken from the ration books. My main concern was hearing the rumour that no bananas would be available until after the war. In spite of the shortages, our family never went short of food. Father had cultivated an allotment garden, which was one of his favourite pastimes, and he regularly brought home the fruits of his labour as the seasons went by. We enjoyed home grown peas, broad beans, new potatoes and carrots, and as the year progressed, cabbage, cauliflower and sprouts. This, together with mother's talent for preparing appetising dishes, ensured that we thoroughly enjoyed our food.

The need for the nation to produce as much home-grown food as possible prompted a 'Dig for Victory' campaign, which saw many people dig up lawns in their back gardens and attempt to grow vegetables. Many parkland areas and green open spaces were used for the same purpose. During these rapidly changing times, the overriding message was to carry on as near to normal as possible. People did so with enthusiasm. Our weekly visit for tea with auntie continued as usual, but mother insisted on taking our own butter and sugar. Mother loved shopping and made the short walk to the shopping centre daily. We were regular customers of the nearby fish and chip shop, and I loved a visit to the sweet shop just around the corner. A large bell clanged overhead as the door was opened, and the sound of someone shuffling along the corridor could be heard, and then suddenly the beaded curtains parted and a charming old lady came into view and served us with a smile. Bread and milk was delivered on a daily basis, by the baker with a horse and cart.

The delivery of milk and bread became quite hazardous as the weather turned bitterly cold. There was an abundance of snow and ice and conditions were so bad, that many people said that it was the worst weather for many years. The gang saw it, not so much as a trying time, but a time for snowball fights and skating on the frozen lake nearby. Unfortunately, this pastime was not without tragedy, as we heard that one lad, although unknown to us, had fallen through the ice and had drowned. Future escapades on the frozen lake were then treated with great caution.

No one had any idea how long the cold weather would last, because weather conditions over the country had to he kept secret, to avoid giving vital information to enemy bomber crews. At that time, only spasmodic incidents were reported, with enemy aircraft sighted over the Thames estuary and eastern Scotland. This was in contrast to the war at sea, where merchant shipping sustained heavy losses, but it was crucial that supplies from America reached this country. Perhaps it was in anticipation of meat shortages that rabbits were put on display in many butcher's shops. They made a rather unappetising sight suspended in the shop window. As a surprise, mother brought one home for us to sample. It was a surprise I could have well done without. None of us could remember eating a rabbit before, and I don't think that we ever ate one again. It wasn't that the taste was at fault, in fact it wasn't at all bad. Perhaps it was the thought of seeing them hopping around in the fields that made the prospect of eating them rather daunting and rabbits were never again on the menu.

Mother became interested in a new programme on the wireless called 'The Kitchen Front' where advice was given on how to make attractive dishes with the rather restricted ingredients available. It was clearly a good programme, for we enjoyed some very good dishes as a result of it. Thoughts of food were suddenly banished as we were required to contemplate how we could respond to an urgent appeal for scrap metal. There was particular emphasis on the need for old bicycles and bedsteads. Our bedsteads were all in use, and father needed his rather old bicycle to ride to his allotment, and follow the hunt. I found it quite amusing, as I imagined the hounds and horses in full cry, followed by father on his bicycle. He was not amused, and was adamant that many people followed the hunt on bicycles. In response to the appeal, we contributed one of our zinc baths, a small one that I had grown out of. Our one remaining large bath was adequate for us. It was a lengthy process to take a bath as saucepans of water had to be heated and then poured into the bath. There was always the possibility of an air raid warning while someone was taking a bath, but, fortunately, during the whole course of the war, there was no warning while I was bathing. Perhaps even more fortunately, there was no air raid warning while mother was in the bath.

The nation continued to enjoy the Saturday night variety shows and other popular programmes on the wireless but we were treated to an additional entertainer who appeared to broadcast from Germany, but who could be clearly heard in this country. He came across as a very unpleasant man and began his regular news bulletins with a sneering introduction 'Germany calling, Germany calling' and followed this with all manner of propaganda, and regularly told us how Germany would quickly win the war. The bulletins were clearly intended to alarm us and cause despondency, but had completely the opposite effect, and gave us considerable amusement. Perhaps he would not have sounded so self satisfied had he known that he was given the name Lord Haw Haw and was looked upon as a comical figure. Mother was not at all impressed when she found me listening to him.

'I don't know why you want to listen to that rubbish,' she snapped.

Perhaps she was annoyed to hear that meat was to be rationed, and wondered whether our Sunday joint of roast beef would be continued.

There were other things to divert our attention as posters appeared in strategic places warning us that 'Careless Talk Costs Lives'. The gang's favourite poster pictured two well proportioned ladies seated in a café and holding a conversation with Hitler and Goering listening in the background. It prompted the gang's comedian to lead a version of our song:

When the Führer says we are the master race
We heil, heil right in the Führer's face

This we sang with a humorous walk and accompanying salute.

A more sober warning came by way of an information film which showed how careless talk by the wife of a sailor led to the sinking of his ship. Those who saw the film would I'm sure be very careful about what they said and who they said it to, when talking about the movements of those we knew in the armed forces. In fact, those in the services spoke very little about their movements, clearly being aware of the potential threat to their safety. Father, working on the railway, would have been aware of any troop movements by train, but said very little.

All was still quiet, apart from sporadic sightings of enemy aircraft in various parts of the country, and so we were able to look forward to a peaceful and enjoyable Easter. There were hot cross buns and plenty of Easter eggs in the shops, which was good to see considering that we thought such things would be in short supply.

For our family a visit to church on Easter day was an obligation, but I didn't mind attending church for the festivals as I enjoyed the hymns.

All places of entertainment did well but, much to our dismay, there were large queues at the cinemas. It seemed that people were determined to enjoy the Easter holiday, not knowing what was around the corner.

Perhaps that was just as well, as we heard that German troops had entered Denmark and also landed in Norway.

A Rude Awakening

After the long periods of inactivity things took a turn for the worse as the Germans quickly made inroads into Belgium and Holland. Rotterdam was almost obliterated by heavy air attacks and, with the Dutch and Belgian opposition completely swept aside, the Germans quickly occupied both countries. Naturally, there was a good deal of speculation about what would happen next.

Our neighbour Bert, who frequently gave us news that he had heard from the pub on the corner, quickly came up with the answer. He announced that Neville Chamberlain had resigned and Winston Churchill had been appointed to lead a coalition government.

It was news that went down well with the gang, as we all thought that Neville Chamberlain was not the strong leader that the country needed.

I think that neighbour Bert was pleased as well, which was gratifying for him, as he was still trying to come to terms with an increase in beer and tobacco prices. Father never made regular visits to the pub, partly due to shift work on the railway, but mother bought bottles of beer for him from the nearby off licence which we called the outdoor beer house. Father also had to pay more for his pipe tobacco which he loved smoking, but I never saw him smoke cigarettes. The same could not be said of Bert, who seemed to have a cigarette in his mouth most of the time, and it was amusing to see it bobbing around on his lips as he spoke. To retain the cigarette in his mouth during the most exciting conversation was an art that he had practised to perfection. It was just as well because he could hardly contain himself when he heard that the Maginot line had been circumvented and that the Germans had made inroads into France.

Winston Churchill promised us blood, toil and tears, and gave notice of hazardous times ahead. This became abundantly clear with news of German forces advancing into Belgium and France which threatened to surround and trap the British force of over three hundred thousand men.

Indeed, the situation that everyone had feared came to pass as German troops surrounded the British forces at the port of Dunkirk. This led to one of the most remarkable operations of the war, and one which was acknowledged to be a miracle of deliverance. Not only was every available naval vessel involved in the action, but hundreds of small boat owners answered an urgent call to help rescue the troops marooned on the beaches.

Father saw exhausted troops glad to be home, as he worked some of the trains transporting them back to their camps. After France fell the nation stood alone to face an armed and trained force across the channel, with the nearest point only 22 miles away. In an important radio speech, Churchill insisted that Hitler would have to break us in this island, or lose the war. He ended a rousing speech by informing us that the battle of France was over, and the battle of Britain was about to begin. We faced this crisis in what we thought was the best possible way: we made a nice cup of tea.

The next gang's meeting on the street corner was a noisy affair, as all loudly contributed their two pennyworth. There was unanimous condemnation of the lack of resistance from the countries that quickly fell, particularly France, where the Maginot line was said to be impregnable. The situation gave cause for concern among our neighbours, but I had the feeling that the gang would see the foreseeable future as an exciting adventure.

Threat of Invasion

The preparations for this adventure began in earnest. There was a round-the-clock effort to produce munitions, aircraft and all manner of weaponry that was so desperately needed in so short a time. Volunteers who were too old to enrol in the services, but who were fit and able, were asked to join the newly formed Local Defence Volunteers later to be renamed The Home Guard.

There was an acute shortage of uniforms and weapons, and the only means of identification was by way of wearing an arm band. During the early days the volunteers drilled with anything that they could lay their hands on: broom sticks, mops, and anything that would temporarily serve as a rifle.

Other defensive preparations proceeded at an astonishing pace. Across the roads leading into the town centre, concrete foundations were prepared in order to anchor large and irregular iron fittings to act as tank traps if and when required. Large wooden posts were sunk into spacious fields and other vulnerable open areas, to deny enemy troop-carrying gliders a potential landing area.

It was envisaged that the Home Guard would deal with an attack by enemy parachute troops, and it was announced that the church bells, which had been silent since the outbreak of war, would be rung to warn of such an attack

Large concrete defensive structures known as pill boxes

were constructed at strategic sites, and could be manned and fully armed if required. All manner of contraptions were assembled on beaches along the south coast to prevent a landing by sea, which made it quite clear that there would be no strolling along the seashore until the end of the war. For good measure, all signposts were removed, so that an advancing enemy force would not know where it was or where it was going. Unfortunately the same situation applied to the local population but this made little difference to us, as only the posh people had cars and it was up to them to ensure that they had in their possession a good map.

Air raid shelters, known as Anderson shelters, which were partially sunk into the ground and protected by sand bags, began to appear in some back gardens. We never opted to have one of these, preferring to take cover under the stairs, as this area was thought to offer the best protection during an air raid The prospect of cold winter nights also proved to be a determining factor.

As we awaited the expected onslaught, Winston Churchill addressed the nation, and asked us to brace ourselves for our duty, and said that if the British Empire and Commonwealth last for a thousand years men will say that this was their finest hour. Those words evidently stirred the nation, for over one million men signed for duty in the Local Defence Volunteers.

There was a shock in store for my sister, as a tax on silk stockings and cosmetics was announced. I couldn't resist the comment that it would cost more to look her best if the invasion came.

Although the times were tense, people made the effort to carry on as normal, and this was certainly the case at school where we were well into the autumn term, Wednesday was sports day. Some kids hated it, but I didn't mind it except during the cricket season. I was quite happy to play football, even though I was never going to be a star, but cricket was a non-starter. I felt that I would never be any good at playing cricket because I was too small, so much so, that when I was required to bat, the large protective pads required made the sight of me running between the wickets quite amusing. When it was the other side's turn to bat, my lack of fielding talent ensured that I was mostly posted out at long on, and sometimes in the teeth of a roaring westerly gale. There were many times when I felt that the five o'clock finish couldn't come quickly enough. There was never an air raid warning during sports period. That would at least have brought proceedings to a premature halt.

In fact air raid warnings had become more frequent, which probably indicated that the Battle of Britain was beginning in earnest.

Attacks were reported on airfields and harbours across the south of England. Our town was surrounded by several airfields, and the one regarded as the most important was the target for an air attack. We heard that damage was quite considerable and several airmen and civilians were killed.

The attacks became more intense, and it was thought that the Germans were attempting to gain air superiority prior to an invasion On the wireless war correspondents gave vivid accounts of the air battles raging over the south of England

Newsreel pictures and the newspapers presented spectacular pictures of the vapour trails left .in the sky by the marauding aircraft. Regular news bulletins reported staggering RAF successes as large numbers of German aircraft were shot down every day, much to the joy of the gang, some of whom were disappointed that the aerial battles took place over the south-eastern part of the country away from our town. The continuing air battles encouraged us to become very interested in aircraft recognition. Most of us had been able to recognise spitfires and hurricanes, and as the raids on the country were stepped up we began to recognise German bombers.

Surprisingly, we were able to see a German bomber close up. The aircraft had been shot down, but not totally destroyed, and was displayed in the car park behind the town hall in an effort to raise money for the Red Cross. It proved to be a very popular attraction.

Quite suddenly, and no doubt due to enormous enemy losses brought about by the bravery and successful action of the RAF pilots, the raids on airfields suddenly abated. The apparent lull in the attacks on airfields was a godsend to the pilots, and to the ground crews who struggled to keep the planes in the air. It also provided an opportunity to repair the damaged runways in an effort to keep the airfields operational.

The sudden cessation of the air attacks made father wonder what Jerry was up to. Jerry being the name used when referring to the Germans, because it was thought that their steel helmets were similar in shape to our bedroom chamber pots, also of the same name.

My sister wasn't the least bit concerned, as she was still coming to terms with more expensive silk stockings and cosmetics. I did have some sympathy for her as it was natural that she wanted to look her best, especially when there were so many servicemen around the town.

This didn't affect mother in the same way of course, but she always kept a small box of face powder to hand, and it was quite amusing to see her brandishing the powder puff and applying the powder quite vigorously, almost to disappear in a cloud of mist.

It didn't take father long to find out what Jerry had been up to, for they had clearly been planning attacks on London which began in earnest. The battle for air superiority prior to an invasion had been won, and Winston Churchill acknowledged, on behalf of the nation, the tremendous debt owed to the fighter pilots, who had achieved a brave and magnificent victory against all odds. The nation breathed a sigh of relief as it was reported that all enemy troops and equipment assembled across the channel had been withdrawn. There were harrowing times ahead though, particularly for Londoners, as the full force of German air power was launched against the city.

The initial raids took place during the day, and were concentrated on and around the docks, where large numbers of incendiaries were dropped. The resulting fires provided a beacon during the hours of darkness to guide the bombers when they returned.

Our relatives, who lived in north London, described in their letters how they looked on grimly as huge areas of docklands were a sea of flames.

The waves of enemy bombers heading towards London certainly did not have things all their own way, They were constantly intercepted by our fighters, and then having arrived over London, were subjected to a sustained onslaught by the anti aircraft defences on the ground.

People of the East End of London found themselves in the front line. I thought of Donald and Joey, the evacuees who had been living next door but who had returned to the city, and I wondered if they had regretted the move. I saw pictures shown in the cinemas of some of the havoc caused by the raids, and vividly remember the sight of an overturned double-decker bus partly submerged in a bomb crater.

On the positive side, the RAF fighter pilots were once again inflicting heavy losses on the German bombers, and it was this that put an end to the daylight raids, but the heavy attacks continued during the hours of darkness. While Londoners bore the brunt of the action, and we assumed that our turn would come, family routines never faltered.

Monday was washing day, a daunting day at any time, but more so when father worked early turn, and I was required to operate the mangle.

There was an extension at the back of our house which we called a glass house. It was mainly the place where father grew and tended his geraniums, but leading off was an area called the wash house, which had a built-in copper, and housed a fearsome looking mangle which appeared as if it would require someone of great strength to rotate the large heavy rollers. That someone was quite frequently myself. Mother began the day early, by lighting a fire under the copper to heat the water.

The clothing and other items to be washed were then immersed and stirred with a large wooden copper stick. Where it was thought necessary, some clothes were treated to a good scrubbing on the pristine wooden scrubbing board, The washing was then rinsed and ready to be fed through the mangle. As I struggled to rotate the large rollers, which squeezed the water out into a large receptacle below, I was reminded of Churchill's promise of toil and sweat. The washing was then pegged on to a clothes line which ran the whole length of the garden, and was propped up to gain the benefit of a brisk westerly wind.

Every family accepted Monday to be washing day, and the sight of all the clothes and sheets billowing on the lines across the gardens reminded me of a large sailing ship.

Mother hoped for what she called a good drying day, so that she could proceed methodically on to the next stage in the procedure which was the ironing. An iron was placed in front of a good roaring fire to gather heat, and when hot enough, the pressing began. Two irons were used, for pressing and reheating alternatively.

Only one task remained. The arrangement of clothes over

a wooden frame which mother referred to as a horse, which was then placed in front of the fire for the clothes to air.

At the end of the day, and with all tasks complete, mother was delighted to announce that she'd washed dried and ironed, tasks which were the aim for every mother on Monday washing day.

It was on a washing day that we first experienced enemy action. Neighbours called us into the garden to observe a large aircraft flying very high overhead. Quite suddenly we heard the sound of distance thuds and news quickly spread that the aircraft had dropped a stick of bombs on open land on the edge of town. Along with many others, we visited the place to see the numerous bomb craters, the sight of which was new to us but a sight that would become far more familiar as time went by. The Red Cross seized the opportunity to take a collection.

Our First Raid

The air raids on London continued night after night. Some people settled down for the night on the platforms of the tube stations, with their sandwiches drinks, pillows and blankets.

The sight of workers picking their way through the rubble following the night's raid to get to work conveyed to the world that Londoners carried on undaunted. The relentless raids on the capital were also of some concern to us, as father frequently found himself on night shift taking a train into the heart of London. Off he went, wearing his smart uniform, and carrying a bag which contained tea, sandwiches and a red and green flag. His pocket watch, with the obligatory chain, rested in his waistcoat pocket, and the important whistle attached by chain to the button hole.

On one particularly hazardous night, during a duty which took him to London, father was convinced that the bombers were after an important bridge, towards which he was heading, which if destroyed would sever a vital route from London to the west.

He explained after he was safely back home that, on approach to the bridge, the train was slowed by signals to a crawl, and eventually halted. The requirement to protect the train by the laying of detonators was suddenly interrupted by the need to dive under the train to shelter from a stick of falling bombs. Fortunately the bridge remained intact, father's duty continued to completion, and he thankfully returned home.

There were occasions though, when delays caused by enemy action resulted in father booking off duty much later than scheduled, which caused us considerable concern.

It was clear that the task of keeping the nation's transport on the move was a hazardous operation.

The blitz on London prompted mother to invite auntie to stay with us to take a break from the continuous bombing, an invitation which she gratefully accepted. On the first night of auntie's stay, father was working nights, as was George, the father next door.

We had all retired to bed quite early, and I was almost asleep when the peace was suddenly shattered by the sound of a low plane roaring over the house tops, followed by the whistling sound of falling bombs. There followed a series of explosions and the sickening sound of falling bricks and masonry. Mother's bedroom door burst open and she bounded along the landing shouting, 'Quick get up! That's bombs!'. We didn't need telling twice and we all made a beeline for the cupboard under the stairs, where several chairs had already been set in readiness for occasions such as this.

After we had settled and looked around, it was quite clear that modesty had no place under wartime conditions, with auntie's hair in curlers, mother with no teeth and me with no trousers. Movement and chatter next door indicated that Rose and June had also taken shelter, and we found it possible to hold a conversation with raised voices.

'That was close,' said Rose.

'I wonder where they came down,' said mother.

'Too close for comfort,' muttered auntie.

'We've got saucepans on our heads,' said Rose.

There was a brief silence while everyone visualised the comical scene, and then followed roars of laughter. There could have been no better way to relieve the tension, but although we all found it amusing, the use of saucepans for protection was an extremely sensible option, We suddenly realised that there had been no air raid warning preceding the attack, and so there would be no all clear siren.

When we thought it quiet and reasonably safe, we ventured into the front garden to see if any passersby had news. Quite a few neighbours had the same idea, and had already found out that the bombs had landed just across the lake at the back of our house. Auntie rounded off the evening with an unexpected and humorous comment when she said that she was invited to spend time with us as a welcome break from the London bombing, but she had been nearer to bombs on her first night in Swindon with us than at any time during the London blitz.

It was said that Londoners had become used to the air raids night after night, and had shown great resilience, and if Hitler thought that he could have brought the country to its knees by the constant bombardment of the city which he referred to as 'Our Beloved London', then he could not have been more mistaken.

This was forcefully demonstrated when, during one of the raids, bombs fell on Buckingham Palace. Far from being viewed as a serious incident, the Queen was said to be very pleased, for having been the bomber's target as so many Londoners had been, she could hold her head high. It was also made very clear that the King and Queen certainly had no plans to leave London. Perhaps it was the Londoners' defiant attitude which led Hitler to believe that the full force of the Luftwaffe should be launched against other targets across Britain. People in a number of cities then experienced the terror and devastation from such raids, none more so than Coventry.

The raid was carried out on the night that my mother had taken me to see a film show in the town hall. The dronc of aircraft passing overhead which began soon after the start of the show, caused quite a distraction. As we emerged after the show, it was clear that large formations of aircraft were passing overhead on what had turned out to be a brilliant moonlit night. If there had been an air raid warning, clearly we had not heard it, and father, who had not been working late, was quick to assure us that the enemy's target was obviously to the north. With that in mind, and with some reluctance, we eventually retired to bed, not knowing until the following day that the people of Coventry had experienced one of the worst raids of the war. It wasn't until our next visit to the cinema that we were able to see newsreel shots of the awful devastation resulting from the raid.

Winston Churchill deemed it necessary to visit the scene, and he was pictured with other civic leaders picking his way through the rubble of Coventry cathedral. The Germans were clearly pleased with the result of the raid and, in one of his broadcasts, Lord Haw Haw promised that other British cities would endure the same experience in the future.

In the weeks that followed, Liverpool, Bristol and Southampton were attacked, and we were frequently aware, following the air raid alerts, of formations of bombers passing over us on their way to targets in the Midlands.

Our town was not completely ignored. One evening the sirens sounded at around seven-thirty in the evening, which concerned us because my sister had been working overtime and would have been on her way home. As she arrived home and opened the front door planes roared overhead and bombs began to fall. Mother quickly ushered sister down the hallway, and we fled to the relative safety of the cupboard under the stairs. A reassuring knock on the wall indicated that Rose and June were also in position with saucepans at the ready. We had often laughed about the saucepans, but on that occasion our saucepans were not too far away.

Another Christmas already

Christmas was more of a low profile occasion, no doubt due to the havoc brought about by the raids, and the need to remain prepared to face whatever came about, but it didn't stop us from enjoying ourselves. Mother continued with the usual ritual of writing cards, and making the puddings and cakes, and produced an unexpected treat of home-made rhubarb wine. I didn't even know that people made rhubarb wine. We all dutifully said that it was very nice, but I must say that it was not received with unbridled enthusiasm.

Part of the holiday entertainment for the gang was a visit to the pictures to see the film 'The Great Dictator', in which Charlie Chaplin gave a humorous and very good portrayal of Hitler.

With the Christmas holiday over, things began to get back to normal. Auntie had returned to London and must have wondered whether it had been the right decision when London experienced its heaviest raid of the blitz. It was concentrated on the City, and the fires were so widespread that it was described as the second great fire of London. Pictures showed the area around the great St Paul's Cathedral as a vast sea of flame, but the cathedral stood out as an inspiring beacon seemingly undamaged. It was quite remarkable that apart from the destruction of Coventry Cathedral, most of these magnificent buildings appeared to have escaped serious damage. At school we experienced the first air raid warning while the class was in session. The air raid shelter was quite close to the school, but confidence in its safety was sadly lacking, for the pupils felt that they stood a better chance of survival by remaining in the school building.

In the event it mattered not because the all clear sounded after a short time, and we all trooped back into the classroom after what was a welcome break from lessons. It was also pleasing when we realised that we had missed algebra.

It was not all smiles however, because the next period was devoted to music. Sometimes during this lesson we were taught to sing, not one of my talents. Other times we were taught how to read music, and there were times when we were obliged to listen to classical music, played on a portable wind up gramophone, brought along and operated with a degree of pride by our ebullient music mistress. She delighted in playing recordings of what she described as descriptive music such as Vaughan William's composition of 'The Wasps'. All went well during the playing of the overture until unfortunately the turntable lost power and slowed, much to the amusement of the class, and a rather embarrassed music mistress began to furiously rewind in order to return to the proper speed. During the hilarity that followed I was one of those singled out for a detention, but as I lived quite close to the school I was not too late arriving home. Others were not so lucky for some pupils had to travel into town by train and bus from the surrounding villages. There were three secondary schools in the town, and two were quite close together in the central area. There was a plan to amalgamate the two schools and house them in a larger complex but unfortunately building work had not started. This led to an extraordinary situation where we were required to walk between the two schools in order to attend lessons. Far from being viewed as an inconvenience, we welcomed the opportunity to take an enjoyable break.

In other cities, where schools had been destroyed as a result of enemy action and where there was also a shortage of teachers, classes often numbered up to fifty pupils, and lessons were held in accommodation which happened to be available at the time, such as church halls, clubs and even pubs.

In such circumstances, we considered ourselves to be quite well off. I considered myself to be even more well off as I lived close enough to school to be able to return home at midday, which enabled me to avoid school dinners. Some pupils said that the school dinners were quite reasonable, but there was nothing like home cooking.

Our school day consisted of four lessons in the morning and three in the afternoon. Obviously some lessons were more acceptable than others, and it goes without saying that the twice weekly period in the gymnasium was one of the most popular. The sessions in the gymnasium were the only times when boys and girls were separated, apart from the sports afternoons.

So far as lessons were concerned, everyone had their likes and dislikes. One of my favourite lessons was geography, and the study of this became even more interesting and enlightening, as the theatres of war spread across Europe and eventually across the world. Strange sounding names of hitherto unheard of places in far-flung parts of the world became known as news bulletins and press reports covered events,. As I grew older I concluded that many of these places would never have become known to me, had there not been a war situation at that time of my schooldays.

We continued to learn as we became familiar with place names in North Africa. We knew that there was a military presence there to protect our Middle East interests and to guard the Suez Canal, and it was this force which was called upon to repel an Italian attack. Italians were not looked upon as fighters by our gang and this view appeared to be vindicated as the Italian attack was repulsed and the British force took an extraordinary large number of prisoners. This operation was followed by an advance across the desert which became so rapid that a furious Hitler was forced to implement measures to try and slow the British advance. He appointed Field Marshal Rommel to take charge, and as our gang had followed the fortunes of high-ranking officers, both English and German, Rommel's reputation as an efficient commander ensured that more attention was focused on events in that part of the world.

Another Raid

Our appreciation of music and culture suddenly blossomed as classical music concerts flourished, not only in London, but also in the provinces. At school we welcomed the visit of an orchestra as we were urged to attend the school's matinee concert. Needless to say, the whole class suddenly became music lovers and quickly gave their names to attend. We then promptly looked to see what lessons we would be missing. On reflection, it became clear that our music mistress had played classical music for us to spark an interest in the music of the masters.

Father was not particularly interested in classical music but enjoyed a programme called 'The Brains Trust'. Questions were sent in by listeners and discussed by well known intellectual members of a panel. Mother was not interested in the programme and always busied herself with sewing and darning and there was plenty of that to do by the way that holes kept appearing in my socks.

On one occasion we were suddenly taken by surprise and the sewing and darning came to a halt by the sound of the air raid sirens As usual we moved into what we hoped was the safety of the cupboard under the stairs. It wasn't long before the sound of aircraft was heard, followed by the sound of falling bombs. At the time I wondered whether it would have been better and safer to have been cold and damp in an outdoor Anderson shelter. rather than our cupboard under the stairs.

I pondered no longer as the all clear sounded, and following mother's usual 'Thank God for that', we moved back into the living room where the sewing and darning continued. We later discovered that the bombs had landed across a park with the last two landing in the area where father had his allotment garden. It was relief all round when he discovered that his garden and shed were unscathed, and we were happy in the knowledge that the seasonal supply of vegetables would continue. It was of course great satisfaction to know that the bombs had not fallen on houses. It was also pleasing to know that raids were being made on targets in Germany and also the occupied countries.

Father had noticed that Wellington bombers frequently passed over the town, and he was of the opinion that they were on their way to bomb the U-boat pens in the French port of Brest as it was there that the U-boats set out in packs to attack shipping in the Atlantic Ocean and English Channel. The Germans attached great importance to operations in the Atlantic and an experienced admiral unknown to us was appointed to lead the offensive. Here was a character new to the gang was followed with interest, for a failure to repel the constant attacks would have had a devastating effect on the war effort. Devastating because the supplies coming from America in large convoys were seen as crucial to the war effort, Winston Churchill was very much aware of this and, in one of his speeches he appealed to the United States with a request, 'Give us the tools and we'll finish the job'.

Whenever Churchill made a speech which was broadcast on the wireless, families across the nation gathered around the fireside to listen. His oratory bore the hallmark of a strong and confident leader. It was as if providence had provided us with crucially important leadership in our country's hour of need.

Although all manner of supplies were being shipped

across the Atlantic there were some people who thought that America should have entered the war. I was never fully supportive of that attitude as I wondered what the American people would have thought, being dragged into a conflict some three thousand miles away. Unfortunately, their efforts to aid us were continually hampered as the convoys came under constant attack by U-boats and sustained heavy losses. There were also other things on which to concentrate our minds, as the Luftwaffe had stepped up attacks on London and other cities in what was described as a spring offensive. London was particularly hard hit and in one raid bombs again fell on Buckingham Palace.

It was quite remarkable that, in the cities where people had experienced continual heavy raids, life carried on as near normal as possible. We saw pictures of office workers climbing over heaps of rubble in an effort to get to work, and buses and trains continued to operate. In the entertainment world the saying that the show must go on proved to be true, as theatre and cinema performances continued as usual, but cinema audiences were notified of an air raid warning by way of a slide projected on to the screen.

Perhaps the best example of carrying on quite normally, whatever the circumstances, was the case of the BBC announcer, who had just begun to read the news when he was interrupted by a loud noise which sounded like an explosion. He paused momentarily and then carried on reading. We learned later that the noise came from a bomb which had landed on or near Broadcasting House and caused considerable damage and quite a few casualties.

An Unexpected Trip

When I had thought that all was going along splendidly, mother suddenly decided that it was time to visit my aunt who had been a school teacher, and who lived in a small town about forty miles away. It was a trip about which I had mixed feelings. I enjoyed the journey on the train, and visiting the fairly large house which was much bigger and grander than our own.

I was always aware during visits that music had played an important part in our family over the years. My cousin, for example, was a very accomplished pianist and gave frequent recitals. I enjoyed watching her play the piano with fluency, swaying to and fro and demonstrating an artistic temperament which added a sense of drama to the music of Bach and Beethoven.

Unfortunately I knew that my turn to play would come, as my aunt had still retained the school teaching instincts of the past, and she always expected me to have a musical piece prepared. My sister had given me a few basic piano lessons, and, following in our family's good musical talents, I had made reasonably good progress, but regarding my potential performance the saying, 'After the Lord Mayor's Show', came to mind.

I managed to get through a brief and rather basic composition which earned a ripple of applause and a nod of approval from a rather proud mother. Unfortunately, I knew that worse was to follow as my aunt always wanted me to recite a poem. I hadn't learned much in the way of poetry at school, and the class comedian's version of 'There Was An Old Man From Gloucester' just wouldn't do. In the end I managed to stumble through some quotations from Shakespeare, which seemed to impress everyone, me included, and I sensed that mother simply bristled with pride. With all of the performances and cultural chores done and dusted, I was able to relax and it was always a joy to wander around the adjoining paddock and feed the chickens.

The real highlight of the visit for me was the tea-time spread. In spite of rationing and shortages, my aunt was able to concoct all manner of delicacies and display them in the manner of a well appointed hotel. As we were on our second cup of tea and feeling exceptionally well fed, mother surveyed the scene and said she wondered what the Minister for Food would have said if he could have seen us. In those days there seemed to be a Minister for most things. With nearly all of the food consumed and a feeling of well being, we made our way to the station to catch the train home.

As the train approached our town, I was surprised to see that barrage balloons had been arranged in a defensive formation to prevent the low flying of enemy aircraft. In the outlying fields there was also a battery of anti-aircraft guns with searchlights. It was satisfying to see additions to Swindon's defence as the raids, which had begun again, were intensifying not only on London, but also on Plymouth, Bristol and Swansea. Bombers frequently flew over our town during the night which we assumed were German bombers on the way to attack targets in the Midlands and the North. On those occasions we didn't think it necessary to shelter under the stairs, but we were very careful to maintain complete blackout and remained ever ready to react to any emergency. Apart from the conventional bombs used during the blitz, a new terror emerged called land mines. They were described as being the size of the post office letterbox and when released drifted down by parachute. The resulting explosion caused an extremely destructive blast, which in some cases obliterated a whole row of terraced houses. The raids across the country resulted in heavy casualties, but it was reported that the surface air raid shelters had generally provided good protection. This observation did little to increase the confidence in the surface shelter which was provided for our use at school.

As time passed and news spread of the deaths of those known to us, killed either on active service, or as a result of air raids, it gave us a grim reminder that we were all in the front line and faced danger at any time, As a result, the general attitude was to live for the day, for you knew not what tomorrow would bring. It was an attitude which led to the deterioration of the moral standard, a standard which was upheld by a large number of people. The 'live for today' attitude, which was frowned upon by the more righteous folk, was more easily understood, as tragic and unexpected events unfolded.

None more so than the loss of HMS *Hood* which was sunk by the *Bismarck* with the loss of nearly all hands on board. This vessel was regarded as one of our most important warships and the devastating news of its sinking stunned us all. The Germans had maintained that the *Bismarck* was the pride and joy of the German Navy and was unsinkable. However, war correspondents reported sustained attacks on the vessel by Royal Navy warships and Swordfish aircraft armed with aerial torpedoes. After a fierce and lengthy sea battle, the *Bismarck* was eventually sunk, much to the relief and joy of us all. Events began to happen thick and fast, and news broke that German forces had invaded Russia. I don't think that this news was greeted with much surprise, bearing in mind the German appetite for continued expansion and aggression. There was, in fact, a rather hopeful feeling that the German military capability would be stretched, having regard to the fact that their forces were also deployed in North Africa.

While all these events were taking place, there was of course the business of carrying on as usual, which involved entertaining and visiting relatives and friends. In this regard, mother had made regular visits on a Wednesday to an aunt who lived on the edge of town. I travelled out by bus to join them after the afternoon school session to arrive just in time for tea. I noticed that mother always took small amounts of butter, sugar and anything pertaining to tea time which was rationed. I do not know if this was a general practice when people visited one another, but mother clearly felt that this was an important condition of our visit.

The downside of the trip was the business of catching the bus back into town. It was always a rather unpleasant experience making our way through the darkness with just a torch for our guidance, particularly if it was wet and windy. We were both thankful that there was never an air raid warning while we were in that unenviable position.

It was quite common at that time to see a lady bus conductor on duty, whose job it was to take fares and issue the tickets. Women had continued to play an important part in the war effort, and those on the buses were affectionately known as 'Clippies'.

In Swindon, buses appeared from all parts of the country, to replace our own town's buses which had been transferred to areas where transport services had been depleted as a result of enemy action.

The father of one of the gang was a bus driver and he would occasionally give us the nod to jump aboard during quiet periods; this enabled us to enjoy the experience of riding on the many types of buses from all parts of the country.

Hazardous Moments

As the Germans advanced deeper into Russia, reports of atrocities against the Russian people began to filter through, particularly against the Jews who seemed to be targeted in all of the occupied countries. The Nazis had a very low opinion of people in the east, which ensured that the last had not been heard of inhuman atrocities.

As if to uplift us Winston Churchill was never slow to rally the nation whenever possible, and he found an opportune moment to promote a V for victory campaign. He encouraged people to paint V for victory signs in strategic places, a move which he thought would be particularly effective in occupied countries. The gang didn't need telling twice, and we went to work brightening up some of the more dreary looking walls and fences. Perhaps our activities were a trifle overdone, and some criticism came our way, but we were sure that the persistent and annoying body of slogan writers, baying for a second front, had also led to the criticism.

I expect a far more acceptable activity, among those we classed as moaners, was our after-school visits to the cinema The latest wartime film showing was 'Target For Tonight'. The storyline followed an RAF crew on a bombing raid over Germany, and those taking part in the film were actual air crew members. This was one of the best films we had seen relating to wartime operations, and crowds flocked to see it.

The film studios were producing and releasing as many films as possible to satisfy the millions who flocked to the cinemas on a weekly basis. Some of our favourites came from the Hollywood film studios and were a mixture of gangster and comedy films. The number of good films being released ensured that our after-school cinema visits became quite frequent. There was one occasion though, when I opted to go straight home, but it proved to be a very unwise decision.

I was nearing home after having left school, when I heard the sound of an approaching aircraft. As the sound grew ominously louder it became clear that the plane was flying at an extremely low altitude. As the plane roared low over the housetops, the policeman on traffic duty was the first to be aware of the danger and roared, 'Get down! Get down!', as a German bomber flew at rooftop level down our street. Some people said that the plane flew so low that you could see the pilot. I was expecting the sound of falling bombs but none came. As we all got to our feet, it was clear that the pilot would have been aware that the street was full of people, including many school children. Some people said that they had heard machine gun fire, but I had not been aware of it. Bullet holes were discovered in some properties in the area but thankfully there had been no casualties.

An anxious looking mother greeted me on arriving home, and she deemed that the unexpected and dangerous incident was deserving of a fruit and cream tea, a treat that was usually kept for special occasions.

My sister had missed the full impact of the event as she had been shopping in the town centre. In any case, she seemed to he more concerned with making the most of her clothing coupons. I was unaware that clothing had been rationed, and possibly would have remained ignorant of the fact, had my sister not made tentative enquiries as to whether mother would use all of her coupons, and whether I would need all of mine. I must have looked reasonably presentable in what I wore or father would certainly have had something to say. It goes without saying that extra coupons went sister's way and she used them most effectively. I suppose that the large military presence in the area had some bearing on the situation.

The news items unfolding were quite grim. Poor old London had been heavily bombed again. The city had taken an awful battering over many months. The raids on London were also very worrying for us when father was booked to take a train to the city, especially having regard to his hazardous experiences there, Other news items were not very encouraging. In North Africa, Rommel was reported to be having some measure of success and, to complete the rather gloomy news, German troops were closing in on Leningrad. Winston Churchill spoke of the wholesale massacre of civilians in Soviet-occupied territories which confirmed the rumours that we had heard.

These were conditions whereby the announcement of something to give us a lift would have been appropriate, but we were targeted by yet another campaign guarding against careless talk. Past campaigns relating to careless talk had been carefully initiated to put the message across in a rather humorous manner. I can recall a poster which depicted a rather amusing situation where two people discussed subjects which could have been of some use to the enemy, yet were blissfully unaware that Hitler and Goering were gleefully listening in the background. The latest campaign was clearly intended to shock. The picture showed survivors clinging to a rubber dingy and sadly looking back at their sinking ship.

Whether the more dramatic approach had the desired effect was most questionable. One lady in the neighbourhood, whose husband served in the Royal Navy, was often heard to announce loudly that her husband, who had been on leave, was off back to join his ship at Portsmouth.

Our New Shelter

We decided that it was time to make the most of what seemed like an Indian summer. Some of us decided to indulge in a sporting activity, while others, including myself, enjoyed a walk into the countryside to search for blackberries, We started off quite confidently, because there was a lad who said that he knew of a place where they could be found in abundance, but when we arrived at the suggested location we found that someone had obviously been there before us and only a few rather unattractive berries remained. Not disheartened we continued the search and we were able to take home a very modest harvest, just about enough for a blackberry pie.

Looking around the countryside it was quite remarkable to see how it had been dramatically transformed since the beginning of the war. Many fields had been ploughed to grow a variety of root crops, and fields of golden corn stretched as far as the eye could see. This was the result of the magnificent work undertaken by the farmers and the thousands of young female volunteers. The name Land Army was given to the many girls who had answered an urgent call to undertake all manner of work on farms and around the countryside.

It was very enjoyable to get out of the town. Perhaps we should have done it more often as it proved to be an excellent way of recharging batteries to fit ourselves for whatever lay ahead. As we moved into the autumn I sensed a feeling of restlessness among the gang and I wondered why. We had long become accustomed to the war situation, and at school we were well into the autumn term. Perhaps there was a need to hear news of a more encouraging nature. The nation had been constantly on the defence as the Germans had advanced across Europe. Bombing missions on German cities had become more frequent, which was encouraging, and we knew that production had been stepped up to produce weapons to take on a more offensive role. Perhaps the unsettled mood was in part brought about by the daunting prospect of end- of-term exams, which loomed in the not too distant future. Generally, I think that we mostly enjoyed school, but exams seemed to come around far too often.

However, my mood was lifted by the dawning of an exciting day heralded by the arrival of our table shelter, which father had applied for months previously. These shelters were allocated to those who had no Anderson shelter in the garden, and we thought table shelters to be a far better prospect with regard to both protection and comfort. The main advantage was the fact that they were assembled and erected inside the house and gave the satisfaction of not having to face inclement weather outside.

Ours was positioned in the middle room and served, not only as a shelter, but also as a dining room table. For large families they were an excellent facility, but our family of four looked a little lost around such a large table. My sister and I discovered that it made a very good table tennis table, and we had some good games playing what we called ping pong.

Its reputation as an air raid shelter was very good. One expert maintained that where the shelter had been properly secured with the occupants inside, the whole thing could be thrown clear following an explosion, and the occupants could survive.

One member of the family found that the shelter had some welcome advantages. The cat loved it and was often to be found curled up on his corner of the mattress which he had commandeered He loved nothing better than a night time air raid warning, where he would stake his corner and enjoy the company of the rest of the family. On one occasion while we were sheltering following an air raid alert, mother said she was sure that the plane she heard flying overhead was a Jerry. I thought that it seemed to be taking a long time to go over, and then we discovered that it was the cat purring and clearly enjoying the moment.

Another Christmas wasn't too far away, but a series of shocks and bad news preceded it. First we were gutted to learn of the loss of one of the Royal Navy's large aircraft carriers the *Ark Royal*. This was followed by news that the Germans were getting ever closer to Moscow, but was tempered slightly by the arrival of the Russian winter which was hoped would hamper military operations and slow down advancing German troops.

Perhaps the greatest shock of all came in early December, when, out of the blue, the Japanese attacked the American naval base at Pearl Harbour in Hawaii. This of course led America into the war, and so what had been a European war, suddenly escalated into a world conflict.

It was quite clear that Winston Churchill was pleased and relieved that America had entered the war, and in acknowledgement of their military might and economic strength, he said in a speech that Britain, the United States and the Soviet Union would teach the enemy a lesson that would not be forgotten in a thousand years.

It was comforting to know that we had the military might of the United States behind us but, remarkably, we were also assured that we had weapons of war in our own households. We were asked to search our homes for old newspapers, magazines and cigarettes packets which could be used in the production of shells, bullets and mines. It prompted father, who was not known for impromptu or humorous comments, to suggest that we look behind the sofa to see if there was a bomb or a mine there.

Christmas 1941 duly arrived but was rather a low-key affair, possibly due to unpalatable events, but mother carried on with the usual traditions and there was no escaping the stirring of the Christmas puddings and making a wish. There was a good table provided in spite of the shortages, but the traditional games of cards and snakes and ladders were edged out in favour of games of table tennis played on our spanking new table shelter.

The news bulletins on the radio reported a mixture of news, some good and some not so good. The tide was beginning to turn against the Germans in Russia, but in North Africa Rommel was making great strides towards Alexandria. Perhaps the most exciting news, particularly for the girls, was that the yanks were coming, and over a short period of time they arrived in our area in large numbers. The girls had looked forward to their arrival, and became very innovative with their efforts to look attractive. They overcame the acute shortage of stockings by covering their legs with sun tan lotion, and cleverly used an eyebrow pencil to indicate a stocking seem down the back of the leg. Men admired such an effective innovation, and us lads who were growing up very quickly in many ways were also alert to the situation.

Unfortunately, the state of being alert was something which appeared to desert our coastal defences, as we heard that two German battleships had made a successful dash through the English Channel and were not spotted until they had reached the Straights of Dover. They had apparently been extensively damaged and undergone repairs in the French port of Brest. This oversight didn't go down very well with the gang, or indeed the nation. An unsuccessful attempt to play the incident down was made by assuring the nation that questions would be asked.

Balloon adrift

Quite suddenly we had an exciting incident to deal with and it was not down to enemy action, A very high wind caused a barrage balloon, situated nearby, to break away from its moorings. It followed an erratic course as it passed over numerous rooftops, and the trailing cable dislodged countless roof tiles and damaged anything else that was in its path. People gathered to watch the balloon's progress until it passed out of sight It was returned to its rightful location a couple of days later, which completed a very successful operation by the emergency services. The unfortunate incident left many householders contemplating quite a substantial financial outlay for the replacement of slates and other rooftop repairs.

Events seemed to follow thick and fast, and it was reported that Singapore had fallen to the Japanese. We were aware of and heard regular news bulletins regarding hostilities in the Far East, but it was the war in Europe which had our undivided attention, quite simply because we were more closely involved. Some men were to become even more closely involved as it was announced that there would be a call up of men up to the age of 45.

The lads wondered whether the war would continue until we reached the age of military service There was no time to dwell on such thoughts though, for it was time once again to visit my aunt who had been a school teacher. I didn't mind visiting her, even though I sometimes had to recite a poem.

There was a surprise in store, for I could see no sign of a good spread which for me was always the high point of the visit. I need not have worried for we were taken out to sample an innovation which was called a British Restaurant. It was a government scheme to provide people with good meals at reasonable prices, and without having to give up coupons from the ration book. The meal was good value for the cost of one shilling. It consisted of meat and two veg, pudding and coffee. We all said that we enjoyed it, but mother intimated that she preferred home cooking. It was as if the Minister for Food agreed for he advised us to eat more potatoes. Apparently white bread was being phased out and replaced with an off white loaf. We all loved potatoes and so were unperturbed by the announcement.

Perhaps the same thing could not be said about the rationing of soap which was brought in to save imported oils.

Although these shortages caused some inconvenience, it was all put into perspective when we heard news of the hardships and suffering endured by the people of Leningrad who were reported to be under continual siege.

It was not all gloomy news though as it was reported that our bombers continued to attack targets in Germany and the gang noted, having an interest in leaders and generals, that Air Marshal Harris had been appointed to lead bomber command. Our belief in his tough reputation was vindicated when he announced that Germany would be attacked day and night. Remembering the raids on London, Coventry, Plymouth and many more cities there was a feeling that at last the tide was turning.

Unfortunately the tide was not turning so well for us at sea. Shipping losses were very heavy as U-boats continued to sink merchant ships bringing vital supplies from the United States.

There was also further bad news for drinkers and smokers, when purchase tax was increased on spirits and cigarettes. Twenty fags went up from one shilling and sixpence to two bob. I didn't hear father complain because he smoked a pipe, but one or two of our older lads used to slip away somewhere for a crafty smoke and so their pocket money would have to stretch a little further.

Under the Shelter

There had been a lengthy lull in air attacks, no doubt because the capabilities of the Luftwaffe had been severely stretched by having to fight on several fronts, which made it very surprising when we heard of a heavy raid on the west country city of Exeter. It later emerged that the raid was in retaliation for RAF raids on historic towns in northern Germany. Unfortunately the retaliation did not end with the raid on Exeter for shortly afterwards they raided the world famous historic city of Bath. The people of Bath were used to seeing a red glow in the sky at night caused by the fires from the raids on Bristol but were shocked to find that flares were being dropped over their city which indicated that they were the target. The city suffered two heavy raids on successive nights causing heavy damage and many casualties. Some people set out well equipped to spend the night in the surrounding fields in anticipation of further raids. Others held the view that they should have remained in the city to protect their homes and aid civil defence personnel.

I am not sure how our family would have reacted under the same circumstances. I think that we would have put our trust in our table shelter and remained at home. It became clear that towns and cities of historic importance were the targets and it subsequently became known that Hitler, in retaliation for the raids on historic towns and cities in northern Germany, had thumbed through a tourist guide and selected Exeter, Bath, Norwich, York and Canterbury as targets for retaliation.

I don't think that Hitler would have classed our town as one of historic importance or a tourist destination, but the night following the raid on Bath, our sirens sounded just as I was about to drop off to sleep.

We dressed quickly and made our way downstairs, with father muttering something along the lines that it must be out turn. We settled into our position under the table shelter, and the cat, thoroughly enjoying the unexpected night time surprise, took up his place in the corner. We carefully ensured that the protective sides of the shelter were properly in place, and then waited to see what ensued.

It wasn't long before the drone of planes could be heard with one flying particularly low over the housetops followed by the thud of bombs dropping some distance away, accompanied by the rattling of the windows and other sundry objects. This prompted mother to ensure that she had the whistle with her in case it was needed. She thought that if the worst came to pass and we found ourselves under a heap of rubble, the whistle would act as a guide for the rescue workers. Shortly afterwards another plane roared overhead and dropped bombs which sounded much closer to us.

I was reminded of the well known saying that you never hear the bomb that is meant for you. We expected the worst and braced ourselves for a hectic and unpleasant night, but the second wave of aircraft never came, and it wasn't too long before the all clear sounded and we all breathed a sigh of relief.

Not all families were so lucky, and one girl told me her story after the raid. Her family, like us, also had a table shelter in which they had put their trust and while they sheltered it appeared that a bomb had landed in the front garden. She saw a cloud of dust enter the room from under the door, and was then momentarily stunned as the fireplace crashed against the side of the shelter. The whole house then collapsed and they were buried under the rubble for around eight hours until they were dug out. Her experience emphasised the importance of ensuring that the protective sides of the shelter were locked in place.

Perhaps the unnerving experiences had given father some thought, for he surprisingly announced that it was about time we went to visit his father. It was usually mother who decided where and when visits should take place. Maybe he had been prompted to visit by news of the constantly expanding airfield, which was adjacent to the bottom of his father's garden. Grandfather lived in a picture postcard country cottage, which I am sure that most people would think an ideal place to live, away from the bustle and vulnerability of the town. It was, however, far from being ideal in many ways.

In our town house, a flick of the switch was all that was required for electric light, but in the cottage, as darkness fell, numerous oil lamps had to be lit. However, the effect of the diffused lighting together with the warmth from the glow of the coal fire was wonderfully comfortable on a cold winter's night and tended to offset any inconvenience.

What was not so wonderful was the effort required if necessary to visit the toilet. This was located in a small shed-like structure at the bottom of the garden, and for a person making a first visit it must have felt like an unwanted adventure. I was extremely thankful that there was no need for me to sit down. The extremely spacious wooden seat had at its centre a daunting black hole, where when looking down there appeared to be a bottomless pit. I felt that it should have been fitted with a safety harness, at least for the use of small people like me.

At night time the use of a chamber pot was a more convenient facility and I should imagine that the chamber pot was used extensively in this cottage. These chamber pots were vital in every household where toilets were located outside of the house. They were usually placed under the bed and were emptied when the beds were made.

The visit to grandfather was very enjoyable, and on exploration, I noticed that the adjoining airfield was a hive of activity, giving the impression that preparations for a more offensive role in wartime operations was well under way.

Quite soon it was time to say goodbye and catch the bus back into town. The act of saying goodbye to grandfather was quite a sad moment for he had long since lost his sight in an unfortunate accident. He would hold my face in his hands for a while, which was his way of attempting to establish some form of recognition and it was a moment where I found it difficult to hold back the tears.

Increased Military Presence

The number of service personnel coming into town had increased considerably, and this was because of the number of army camps and airfields that had sprung up around the town in a remarkably short time. Certainly there was an increase in army vehicles that we had not seen before. The peace and quiet was often shattered as convoys of tanks made their way down our street. Although somewhat noisy, they were quite small and were known as Bren gun carriers. They did not look suitably armed to be involved in battle, but were used for moving equipment and transporting personnel.

The increase in military presence had a beneficial effect on the cinemas, dance halls and pubs, as many people flocked to these venues for their entertainment. Perhaps it was the need to keep military personnel occupied that prompted the government to announce that cinemas could open on Sundays.That had little effect on our family, because mother held the view that there was plenty of time to go to the pictures during the rest of the week. The only place that we visited on a Sunday was church.

The huge military presence around the town was encouraging to see, but it made me wonder whether this would make us a target for enemy bombers. Fortunately the raids by the Luftwaffe had become few and far between, but a number of incidents proved that bombers were still available for making surprise attacks. So far as our town was concerned, we found it quite unbelievable, yet very thankful that we had not become a target for very concentrated raids. Swindon produced much in the way of armaments and was an important railway junction and home to a large railway works. Perhaps we had escaped the blitz completely for there had not been concentrated raids on cities for quite some time.

However, one day at lunchtime the sirens sounded, and it was the first air raid warning during daylight hours for a long while, and gave some cause for concern. We settled into our table shelter together with the cat, who was late taking up his position, no doubt surprised by such a move taking place during daylight hours. Quite soon an aircraft roared overhead and dropped a stick of bombs which sounded as though they had landed some distance away. Shortly afterwards the All- Clear sounded. It appeared that only one aircraft had been involved in the attack, and these raids became known as hit and run attacks. There followed, as usual, a neighbour's inquest, and Bert was of the opinion that the target was a factory in the north of the town which produced aircraft parts, but in fact the target appeared to have been the gas works, as we later heard that a gas holder had been destroyed. Some observers said that the area had been raked with machine gun fire.

There were other unfortunate surprises around the corner, but they had nothing to do with air raids. It was announced that sweets and chocolate were to be rationed. I loved the plain dark chocolate, Milky Ways, fruit drops and bulls eyes. The sweet shop in our street was run by a dear old lady. She looked a diminutive figure as she stood behind the counter in front of shelves full of jars of sweets. My pennyworth of fruit drops were weighed and then poured into a three cornered bag which was flipped over a couple of times and placed into eager, outstretched hands.

The Americans who had become established in camps around the town were seen in great numbers. Some roared around in a small and quick military vehicle called a Jeep, which was said to be a great asset transporting personnel and equipment.

Large tanks also came down the street in convoy. They were much bigger and more menacing than the small Bren gun carriers, and they did more damage to the road surface.

Of more interest to us was the fact that the troops in the passing vehicles threw chewing gum towards us which was gratefully received. This pleasant gesture ensured that we were on frequent alert to hear the sound of approaching tanks. Some of the largest bombers we had ever seen soon arrived at one of the largest airfields near the town. They were called flying fortresses which was a perfect description, for when operational, they made an impressive and spectacular sight as they roared in formation over the town on their way to attack targets in Germany. The Fortress bombers attacked mostly during daylight hours, while RAF bombers continued the night time raids.

Clearly buoyed by the apparent success of this combination Bomber Harris, the commander-in-chief, was prompted to announce a stern warning to the Germans.

'We shall be coming every night and every day': a warning that went down very well, not only with the gang, but with everyone involved in the war effort. Quite suddenly we were reminded once again that the Luftwaffe still had planes available to make raids on this country. We were enjoying a quiet Saturday morning, having had a leisurely breakfast and, as father was working evening shifts, the whole family had been able to sit down together. The rag and bone man could be heard shouting in the distance, the weather was sunny and settled, and everything pointed to a relaxing day.

Suddenly and surprisingly the sound of the air raid sirens brought us back down to earth, and we took our place under the table shelter, joyfully preceded by a purring cat, who had enjoyed his breakfast and couldn't believe his luck as he settled into his comfortable corner.

The unusual daylight warning prompted father and various neighbours to carry out somewhat risky observations from the back garden.

It wasn't long before the sound of a plane was heard accompanied by heavy gunfire from the ground batteries. From the frustrating conversations that ensued, it seemed that the plane was flying at a far greater height than usual, and the exploding shells from the gunfire were falling quite short of the target. Further conversation on this matter was rudely interrupted by the sound of falling bombs. Father quickly abandoned his observation post, and with a warning shout to all concerned, moved as quickly as I had seen him move to take his place under the table shelter. The extraordinary sound of bombs falling from such a great height and which took a considerable time to hit the target, gave us some very anxious moments, before a bomb landed quite close with an ear shattering explosion which shook everything to its foundations.

I breathed a sigh of relief that we were still all in one piece, but was surprised to see that the cat was still enjoying his unscheduled nap seemingly unperturbed. Fortunately the raid was short lived and life once again returned to normal. Our neighbour had cause to remember the day for another unfortunate reason. He had chosen not to make a dive for cover in the house as the bombs fell, but rather fell flat in the garden. It was not a wise decision as he soiled his best suit which he was wearing because he had to attend an important event later in the day. Unfortunately further unpleasant surprises befell him and ourselves later in the day. The evening began with a severe electrical storm, with almost continual lightning and torrential rain. Soon afterwards mother stepped into the kitchen and discovered that it had been flooded to a depth of around six inches. Our neighbour also stepped into his flooded kitchen, and to his annoyance soiled his best suit for the second time in one day.

Although our neighbour George had found it difficult to retain a smart appearance, the same problem did not apply to the Land Army girls who had been issued with new uniforms. They cut a dashing figure in green pullovers, brown breeches and smart hats which they obviously wore with pride. Not surprisingly, for they were doing sterling work on the land.

Quite appropriately it was Harvest Festival once again, and how quickly that had come around. I enjoyed the festivals, especially at harvest time when we sang 'We Plough The Fields And Scatter' and 'Let Us With A Gladsome Mind Praise The Lord For He Is Kind'. The choir of some fourteen boys and ten men led the singing with gusto which was a joy. I also remember the glorious line from the psalm as we sang 'The Valleys Shall Be So Thick With Corn That They Shall Laugh And Sing'.

Quite a lot of people attended churches at the time, and although people had their own ways of dealing with the stressful conditions, albeit without religious convictions, the church still had an important part to play. There were those who appeared to be oblivious to the season of harvest and were more concerned with calling for the immediate launching of a second front. Slogans such as 'Second Front Now' began appearing on walls and fences around the town, but most people, quite sensibly, thought that an operation of such magnitude would require meticulous planning and plenty of time to prepare, and concluded that a second front was some considerable time away.

There were, however, other encouraging signs of an offensive nature. The RAF began to step up raids on German cities, and in the cinema we watched pictures taken of the result of an astonishing raid on Cologne which had been attacked by one thousand bombers. Reconnaissance photographs, which later appeared in the press, showed the awful extent of the destruction.

There soon followed another one thousand bomber raid which targeted the city of Bremen, and it became clear that the appointment of the nicknamed 'Bomber Harris' was having a devastating effect.

The American forces, who had arrived in great numbers, had made themselves very much at home. They also played their part in keeping up the people's spirits. A good example of this occurred following an air raid alert, which sounded as I was walking through a central park. American servicemen, who were playing baseball, took cover with myself and other passersby in the nearby air raid shelter. Conversation was at a minimum as British reserve and stiff upper lip prevailed. Quite suddenly the Americans began to sing 'She'll Be Coming Round The Mountain' and invited us all to join in. It wasn't long before all signs of reserve had disappeared as we sang one chorus after another. Perhaps it was just as well that there was no sound of falling bombs or gunfire to mar the occasion, and when the all clear sounded it became apparent that the Americans felt that it had been a job well done.

This was a time when the country seemed to be in a buoyant mood, a feeling further boosted by news of a major attack on German forces in North Africa. The sheer scale and ferocity of the attack was vividly described by war correspondents, but the newsreel pictures of the preceding artillery barrage, which began during the hours of darkness ,were truly astonishing. This preceded a tremendous battle which resulted in a breakthrough and a speedy advance across the desert, giving great cause for optimism. Indeed it proved to be a turning point in the war which eventually led to the defeat of the Germans in North Africa. Our gang always expected that Monty would do it, and we joined in the nation's celebrations. Winston Churchill ordered that the church bells, which had been silent since the start of the war, should be rung to mark the occasion.

He also made one of his highly regarded speeches, which often left us not knowing what he was talking about: 'This is not the end. It is not even the beginning of the end. But it is perhaps the end of the beginning.'

Tide Turning

As time passed it became clear that the Luftwaffe had hardly entered British skies, yet Bomber Command together with American aircraft, had pounded German cities by day and by night.

There was also good news that the Russians had surrounded Stalingrad following fierce counter attacks. A look at the map of the Soviet Union showed how far and how quickly the German forces had advanced, not only to Stalingrad, but as far as Leningrad where the city was under siege and the population faced starvation. There were reports of atrocities carried out by the advancing troops on the civilian population, particularly where people were imprisoned in compounds that the Germans had constructed which were known as concentration camps. The Jews were especially targeted. Winston Churchill, in one of his speeches, declared that the perpetrators would face retribution.

The next gang's meeting on the street corner was not about the progress of the war, but the campaign to stop the spread of sexual diseases, which had apparently become rampant. I suppose it was really no surprise, given the number of service personnel in the country, the blackout conditions and the 'live for today' attitude which prevailed at the time. As the blackout conditions had not kept us indoors, we were able to see how illicit and secret meetings took place in dark alleys and behind telegraph poles. Some worried dignitaries, who were witnessing a long and trusted moral standard somewhat deteriorate, suggested that more entertainment for the troops might be a way of reducing infections. There were some in authority who thought that unless effective steps were taken to eradicate sexual diseases, the war effort would be adversely affected. Time eventually proved that such thoughts were completely unfounded.

Of much more interest to us was the release of new films scheduled to arrive in our cinemas in the run up to Christmas. There was comedy provided by the wonderful Will Hay with a humorous portrayal of Hitler in 'The Goose Steps Out'. The film, depicting the successful evacuation of Dunkirk, made a good dramatic contribution. Perhaps the most talked about and well known film starred Noel Coward and John Mills in 'In Which We Serve' which portrayed the agonising experience of survivors from a naval vessel sunk by enemy action, and helplessly adrift in a rubber dingy. My favourite film was 'Went The Day Well', which told the story of life in a northern village which was secretly taken over by German troops, who then had to contend with the ingenious efforts of the villagers who were determined to get a message to the outside world. Many British-made films were released at that time but many more came from America and the stars were well known here.

While British producers made excellent dramatic films, they were unable to match the large-scale musicals in which the Americans excelled.

One popular American star was Bette Davis, who often portrayed scheming, dislikeable characters in the many films that she made.

These stars, and many more, continued to attract capacity houses in cinemas which were the main venues of entertainment during those harrowing times.

Another Christmas had come around and was enlivened

by the visit of my aunt who had come down from London. She loved visiting us, and her infectious laughter ensured that we all had a very merry Christmas. Apart from the traditional games of Ludo and Snakes and Ladders, we had become adept at playing table tennis on our indoor table shelter, but my aunt, always game for a laugh, introduced us to an hilarious game called 'Mrs Mackenzie's Dead'. Perhaps the title didn't indicate a game of such hilarity, but that's exactly what it was.

It began with a question and answer with the person sitting next to you:

'Mrs Mackenzie's dead.'

'Oh yes. How did she die?'

'With one shut eye end her nose all awry.'

This information was passed from person to person until all were sitting, and attempting to stifle laughter, with one closed eye and screwed up noses. The rounds continued as the leader added more ingenious afflictions, until the game was brought to an early conclusion with the participants helpless with laughter.

The evening always ended with a sing-song around the piano. My limited capabilities as a pianist were just about good enough for those present to be able to recognise the tune being played. Perhaps mother's home-made rhubarb wine added impetus to the proceedings, but whatever the reason a rattling good sing-along was had by all.

It was at such times where food appeared to be plentiful and the spirits high, that it was difficult to believe that there was a war on, until succeeding news bulletins brought us swiftly back to earth.

The year 1943 started with good news that the Russians had almost won the battle for Stalingrad, and there was also hope for Leningrad whose citizens were under siege and where people had died from starvation. It was not all good news, as a lone German aircraft carried out the first attack on London for around six months. A school was bombed and many children were killed. It was therefore gratifying to hear that heavy raids were being made on Germany, with Berlin being a particular target. Father, on his visits to his allotment garden, said that he had noticed that Wellington bombers were once more flying over the town no doubt to continue the attacks on the French ports of Brest and Lorient. He had seen such activity in the past and he thought that attacks were being stepped up to win the war in the Atlantic Ocean, so that supplies could reach us from America unhindered. Father was not usually one to hold forth on a subject with enthusiasm, as he tended to sit and listen from behind his pipe, but of this observation he was very confident, and as events unfolded he was proved to be right.

There was great satisfaction over the news that the Russians had been victorious at Stalingrad and also because it appeared that the tide of war in the Russian zone was turning in their favour. The good news lifted spirits, but perhaps the approach of spring also had something to do with it. It seemed that mother was in a nostalgic mood, for at teatime, on one of those rare occasions when we were all able to sit down together, she began to look back and assess how we had coped with the changing conditions, and how we would face the future. We decided that we had coped very well with the wartime conditions up to that date, and were determined that more of the same was the way forward.

Mother had become aware that many goods were in short supply, not only clothes and furniture, but household items as well. It was accepted that queuing for some things had become a way of life, but acute shortages had driven many goods under the counter.

Cigarettes were hard to come by, and batteries which

were necessary for torches to help us cope with the blackout, were also in short supply. As more goods were kept under the counter, and made available for regular customers, it was an advantage to keep up a good rapport and be on good terms with the shopkeeper.

Although there was a shortage of goods and some foods, there was never a shortage of campaigns and promotions. We were all asked to 'Dig For Victory' and to grow vegetables in our back gardens. Father quickly made it clear that he would not dig up the lawn in our garden; he maintained that his constant supply of vegetables which he grew on his allotment was more than adequate to justify our response to the campaign.

Some people not only sacrificed flowers for vegetables, but also went a step further and kept chickens, but thankfully there were no chickens in close proximity to us.

A campaign called 'Wings For Victory' was very well supported in an effort to raise money to build more bombers. The constant raids on German cities, with the resultant losses, had hastened the need for replacements. Pictures appeared in the press of bombers alongside famous London landmarks, and in our town I can recall the sight of a Stirling bomber displayed at the back of our town hall. The campaign produced dramatic results and raised huge sums of money. It was at that time that big efforts were made to increase production and an urgent request was made for more women to make themselves available for work.

The festival of Easter was greeted by the ringing of church bells which had been silent since the beginning of the war. They had been held in readiness to warn of an invasion by paratroopers, but the threat of invasion had long since faded, and it was quite an uplifting feeling to hear the bells again. Not everyone was pleased about it. Some people had moaned about the bells rudely awakening them from their lie-in and had welcomed the prohibition, Some bells had to be repaired and refurbished before they could be brought back into use, having not been rung for such a long time.

It was revealed that road casualties had been high due to the blackout conditions. The gang had not been particularly affected by it, and mother had coped quite admirably with the use of a torch whenever she ventured out in the dark. Some people experienced difficulties and incredible stories did the rounds. It was reported that a person alighted from a train at Bath in the darkness and, thinking it was the platform, she stepped on to the parapet of the bridge which crossed the river adjacent to the station and then fell into the river. It was a story that took some believing but some very odd things happened at the time.

Holidays as usual

Spring had sprung and it was nice to welcome the lighter nights and the better weather, and to see the daffodils in the garden. Not exactly a host of dancing daffodils, but enough to make a presentable showing in our rather small garden. However, it was not all plain sailing because it was time for the budget. As usual all the old faithful targets were hit. Beer, wine and spirits were to cost more, as was tobacco and cigarettes. Bert next door liked a pint but seemed resigned to the ever increasing cost. Father on the other hand was not so much of a drinker, but he loved to smoke his pipe, and I imagined that nothing would ever put him off.

The cost of going to the pictures was also increased, but had little effect on attendances as a visit to the cinema was the main and most popular entertainment at the time, and continued to be so during the whole course of the war.

We were heartened by a sudden announcement that the ban on the ringing of church bells was to be lifted. It was a moment to savour as it endorsed the view of most people that an enemy invasion was deemed to be out of the question. Indeed, most thoughts turned towards where an Allied invasion would take place. A landing had already been made on the French coast at Dieppe. The purpose of the landing was never made clear, but it may have been an operation to test the defences with a forthcoming second front in mind. Whatever the reason the raid was not regarded as a success.

One member of the gang, who had surprisingly come out with pearls of wisdom in the past, was of the opinion that a landing in Italy was the best option, in spite of calls for an immediate invasion across the channel.

Quite remarkably it began to look like an accurate prediction as Sicily was heavily bombed as if to prepare the way. We came to the conclusion that only time would tell if he was right, and meanwhile there was the school summer holiday to look forward to.

The air attacks on the country had become few and far between as the Luftwaffe was required elsewhere. This prompted countless outdoor activities during the summer months. Especially enjoyable were events called 'holidays at home'. Our town hosted quite a few of these events which were intended primarily to encourage people to stay at home. There was always a fairground attraction and donkey rides were available. Brass bands and other entertainments proved to make the events extremely popular.

If the purpose was to encourage people to stay at home, it was unsuccessful. Many families made day trips to the seaside, It was not possible to access beaches on the south coast, as they were looked on as the first line of defence and were home to barbed wire and all manner of obstacles in an attempt to foil an enemy landing. Our family always took a day trip to a resort such as Weston-super-Mare.

An all-day trip required a substantial amount of food to be taken for picnic lunch and tea on the beach, and a case was duly packed with sandwiches, cakes and fruit together with flasks of tea.

Following the exciting arrival and establishing a position on the beach, the first task was to ascertain whether the tide was on the way in or unfortunately on the way out. If it was the latter, the sea seemed to take its leave quite quickly and was soon a rather vague vision on the distant horizon. Fortunately we were nearly always lucky and were able to welcome the incoming tide. I could never understand why mother had a most extraordinary urge to sit as close to the sea as possible for when it advanced up the beach we had to fall back to another position, albeit a temporary one.

I was never one for splashing around in the sea, neither was my sister. A quick paddle, if the water was not too cold, and a ride in a coach pulled by one of the donkeys was all that we required to complete an enjoyable day. The return to the station was made easier by not having to handle a fully laden case, and we arrived early to be in a good position to take on what was always an inevitable scramble for seats as the train came to a halt alongside the crowded platform.

Hats and buckets flew in the scramble, but remarkably everyone appeared to find a seat on the non-corridor train. It was just as well that the initial trip was only twenty miles to the main station where we had to change on to an express train to complete our journey.

The seaside trip was in no way a means to take a break from the wartime situation, for although the large-scale raids on the country had long since subsided, there was always the chance that loan raiders would make sporadic attacks.

The destruction wrought by the blitz was all too evident as the train passed through areas which had borne the brunt of the attacks. Many churches had been reduced to a shell with only outside walls remaining. Rows of terraced houses were in ruins, brought about by the fearsome weapon known as the land mine which floated to earth by parachute and caused maximum destruction.

Apart from the trips to the coast through war-torn areas other ideas began to emerge. Some of my school friends, who were obviously enjoying the holiday decided that they would like to go camping. Parents unfortunately put a damper on the idea, suggesting that the open countryside was not the safest place to camp, where all manner of military manoeuvres took place

Not to be defeated the lads pitched a tent on the lawn of a friend's large house, after his parents gave the idea their blessing. There were many other activities which we enjoyed, such as football and treks to the surrounding downs and forests, complete with sandwiches, cakes and bottles of lemonade. Not too many of us played cricket. I certainly didn't remember my experience on the school playing fields.

While exploring the countryside we frequently encountered American service personnel on tanks and Jeeps, and as usual we were grateful for the chewing gum which was tossed in our direction. Relations between the civilian population and the American servicemen were very good in our area, but news broke of serious unrest in the north of the country, where disturbances had resulted in many casualties. We had not completely escaped that kind of trouble in our town, which sometimes arose between British and American servicemen as they competed for partners in the town's dance halls.

Perhaps their minds were eventually concentrated elsewhere as raids on Germany by their own Flying Fortresses and the RAF were dramatically stepped up and there began a huge drive to produce aircraft and munitions. Men over 65 and women without children were expected to work, and music from the BBC was relayed into factories in an effort to keep up the momentum. Variety shows were also staged during the lunchtime breaks where professional artists entertained. All the shows were broadcast and made entertaining listening. Amateur entertainers were not overlooked and were given the opportunity to broadcast a show every Wednesday which was entitled 'Works Wonders'. It was perhaps an over-ambitious title, as the sound of brass bands left a little to be desired. Most brass bands came from the north, and the best choirs came from Wales. The shows were very popular and provided first class opportunities for the amateurs to showcase their talents.

The end of the school holidays came round very quickly. There was a fresh and pleasant feeling about the start of the new term, and there was also something else in the air. It was clear that the optimistic mood of the nation had found its way into the classroom, and there was a twinkle in the eye of the headmaster as he strode into the hall with brisk movement and gown flowing to take the assembly. The music mistress, poised at the ready over the piano, was almost wearing a smile as she accompanied a particularly robust singing of the morning hymn. The air of a new dawn continued with the issue of pristine writing blocks, new pencils, pens and books.

The air of a new dawn also continued on the war front, with a large-scale landing on the island of Sicily, where Italian troops showed scant regard for stubborn resistance and surrendered in their thousands. This must have infuriated Hitler and it wasn't too long before Mussolini was stripped of his office. Meanwhile bombing raids continued on the Italian mainland and military installations on the outskirts of Rome were attacked. This led to an appeal by the Pope for the raids on the city to be discontinued, and fervently hoped that what he described as the eternal city would be recognised as unique.

The same could not be said of the city of Hamburg which had suffered its heaviest raid of the war. The newsreel pictures of the fires caused by the many incendiary bombs were quite horrendous, and generated some sympathy for those below. It was also a potent reminder of how the fortunes of war had changed. Our household routine hadn't altered much, but it was noticeable that neighbourly communications had become more efficient, so that when commodities such as fish, which was not rationed, and the luxury of sausages became available, the news was passed quickly from neighbour to neighbour, and off we went at speed to join the queue. The art of queuing, which had long become an accepted way of life had, I suspected, become quite enjoyable, as choice bits of information and scandal were divulged and heartily discussed.

The gang's routine hadn't changed much either, but there were more interesting things to see. Military vehicles were around in greater numbers. Large tanks often came down the street and sometimes played havoc with the road service. The Jeeps which we had seen before, roared around transporting goods and personnel from place to place, and large army lorries carrying American troops often passed by, but unfortunately too quickly for the traditional throwing of chewing gum. Aircraft constantly flew overhead as the raids on Germany intensified. Formations of American Fortresses made a spectacular sight as did the RAF Lancaster bombers, and they began to reach deeper and deeper into the heart of Germany. There was also tremendous activity on the Russian front as Russian troops continued to push the Germans back and threaten to surround and trap large numbers. The pendulum had certainly swung in favour of the Russians and things were moving apace.

Lord Haw Haw, the traitor who had been most vociferous broadcasting all manner of propaganda from Germany, was uncharacteristically quiet. Not surprisingly, as there had been little to boast about as the war had swung dramatically in favour of the Allies. He did, though, suddenly appear to be revitalised, and spoke most enthusiastically about a German secret weapon, which he maintained would cause great destruction and lead Germany to victory. If the pronouncement was intended to demoralise the people it had little effect; in fact most people found him to be most amusing.

There was no time to be despondent during that time as there was great news of a landing on the toe of Italy. As if to mark the occasion, the landing coincided with the anniversary of the declaration of war. The wise member of the gang, who had predicted a landing in Italy, thoroughly milked the occasion with several renderings of 'I told you so' which made us come to the conclusion, but not too enthusiastically, that we should hold him in higher esteem.

The gang's hunch about the Italians' lack of fight proved to be correct as the landing in Italy soon brought about an Italian surrender and they signed an armistice. We thought that this cave-in must have left Hitler absolutely fuming, as it was then up to German forces to stem the Allied advance up through Italy. Bearing in mind the Russian successes on the Eastern front, the Germans must have felt very apprehensive about a further spread of manpower. Be that as it may, it did not stop them putting up a very strong resistance, which made the advance up through Italy slower than was envisaged.

Quite a few things were happening on the home front. We were advised once again of a manpower shortage, and boys of sixteen and seventeen years of age were called to work in the pits. There was yet another 'Dig For Victory' campaign which didn't go down very well with father or other allotment garden holders. The landscape had dramatically changed as hedgerows had been removed and fields given over to the cultivation of all manner of crops in an effort to make the nation as self-supporting as possible. Although this was never likely to be achieved, it was reported that food production had doubled.

Good reports continued to come from the Russian front where large numbers of German troops were encircled and taken prisoner. I would not have liked to have been in their shoes as they contemplated what retribution would come their way, having regard to the atrocities and suffering inflicted on the Russian people, when the Germans had speedily advanced into Russia.

The situation was quite the reverse in Italy where heavy rain and mud had halted the allied advance.

There was concern, once again, about what was described as the declining standard of morality. There had been a considerable amount of unease in the past which had caused church leaders to express the need for greater self control. It was an appeal which went unheeded as members of the gang who constantly experienced life on the street corner, were well aware. The air attacks on Germany were relentless, and Hitler promised retaliation for what he called the Reich bombing terror. Perhaps he should have been reminded of the terror inflicted on the citizens of London, Coventry and Plymouth.

Entertainment Boom

The evenings were drawing in again, but one of the nice things about the winter evenings was the feeling of warmth from the glowing embers of the coal fire which had roared triumphantly throughout the day, but tended to look a rather spent force as the evening approached. It was then that the opportunity to make toast was at its best. My sister or myself were usually delegated to carry out the task which involved holding a slice of bread on the end of a large fork in front of the fire. I was not a good toast maker. The first efforts often resulted in the bread being burned to a cinder before I ascertained the correct distance to hold the bread from the fire. It was good that we all loved toast as it made quite a pleasant and easy meal for tea, but care had to he taken not to spread on too much of the butter ration.

The downside of the winter evenings for me was the increased amount of homework and revision required for the end of term exams, given that there was so much going on during the approach to Christmas in the entertainment world, particularly in the cinemas where new films were released.

An extraordinary number of people went to the cinemas and it was said that twenty five to thirty million tickets were sold every week. Many films were morale-boosting, such as 'Desert Victory' which recounted the successful North African campaign, and the remarkable film called 'Fires Were Started' which followed life in a fire station at the height of the London blitz, and where all the roles were played by real firemen. The American offering at the time was 'The Battle Of Midway' which gave an insight into the hostilities in the Far East. It is perhaps an unfortunate thing to admit, but although we were constantly informed by news bulletins and press reports of events in the Far East, it was something that we didn't watch closely, as the need to keep abreast of events in Europe required the most concentration, and so it was good to see American films which kept us in touch with events in the Far East.

Many screen stars became household names. Bette Davis and Joan Crawford were known for their mostly dramatic and treacherous roles, while Betty Grable was known more for her shapely legs than for her acting ability. Humphrey Bogart proved to be a popular star in the film 'Casablanca'.

Apart from the popularity of the cinema, dancing was enjoying a boom and a lively routine called jitterbugging swept the nation. It was a dance routine enjoyed by the young at heart, for fitness and mobility were the main qualifications required.The boom in dancing was, in the main, brought about by what was known as the Big Band sound, and the American dance bands led the way. So many names come to mind: Woody Herman, Artie Shaw, Tommy Dorsey, Harry James, but the most popular and certainly the most famous was Glen Miller. He recorded such outstanding pieces as 'Moonlight Serenade',' American Patrol', 'Opus One' and many more. Good singers began to emerge, and Bing Crosby, who had long been an established vocalist, found himself rivalled by up and coming singer Frank Sinatra, who, when singing his songs, had the ability to make the young girls swoon.

Classical music was also popular and, where there was no adequate concert hall available as a result of the bombing, the concerts were held in cathedrals. In spite of all the entertainment attractions, I did actually manage to complete enough revision and homework which enabled me to just about scrape through the exams, but the results were no more than average and it was a case of 'must do better'.

As we approached Christmas 1943 mother had heard that turkeys would be in short supply but was not unduly concerned for we were unable to afford one anyway, and we were quite happy with chicken or beef and the supply of good vegetables from father's allotment garden. Also, it would be remiss of me not to mention mother's excellent home-made Christmas puddings which completed the menus and made for some hearty eating over the Christmas period.

Christmas was a very enjoyable time as usual. My aunt had come down from London again, which was good for quite a few laughs, and her liking for a good sing-along ensured that the old piano was put to good use. There were also frequent games of table tennis played on our large table shelter, which had not been used for what it was intended for some considerable time, as the Luftwaffe had been busy elsewhere. My sister might have been good at making the toast, but I won most of the table tennis games.

The entertainment venues, particularly the dance halls, were busy because of the continued increase in the military personnel around the town, but unfortunately scuffles often broke out as the British and American soldiers were in competition for partners. However, none of this could overshadow the optimistic mood which prevailed as we looked towards the new year which we thought may herald the long-awaited second front.

A Monastery Destroyed

The start of the 1944 was very encouraging, We as a family never marked new year's eve with any celebration.In fact, more often than not, we were in bed when the clock struck twelve, but nevertheless there were plenty of things to be excited about. The Russians had the Germans in full retreat along large sections of the Russian front, the RAF was carrying out heavy raids on German cities, and there was one particular piece of news which pleased the gang. We heard that the battleship *Scharnhorst* had been sunk. This warship was one of the two ships which made a successful dash through the English Channel to the comparative safety of the German ports. We were at the time quite annoyed that such a daring attempt had been successful, and thought that our coastal defences must have been asleep, so it was very gratifying to hear of the sinking. Russian successes continued and at last the long siege of Leningrad came to an end.

As if to spoil the mood of optimism, London was attacked for the first time in many months, and showed us that although the Luftwaffe had been severely stretched, we could never feel completely free from air attacks. Perhaps we had felt safe in our school because it had been many months since we had practised an emergency evacuation to the air raid shelter. This was a pity because the exercise had always made a nice break from lessons. Although the mood of optimism in the country continued, things were not all going our way. The Allied advance up through Italy had been halted at a place called Monte Cassino. The newsreel shots gave us some idea of the problems involved. The Germans held a hilltop location which gave them extremely good observation of troop movements below. To further complicate the problem, a monastery dominated the summit. There appeared to be much deliberation before the resultant action taken provided one of the most spectacular newsreel shots of the war. In a very heavy raid the bombs rained down on the hilltop location with such intensity that little was left standing after the bombers had left and the monastery had been completely destroyed.

A very intense debate followed and questions were asked whether such action had been necessary, having regard to the religious significance. I sensed a certain amount of misgiving among some of the older people, even though the allied commander had insisted that such action was necessary. There was no such foreboding at the street corner meeting of the gang and the action was endorsed one hundred per cent.

News of an extraordinary nature took our attention from Italy to the Far East, where we learned that Japanese pilots were carrying out suicide attacks by crashing their aircraft into selected targets. This, of course, dramatically improved the accuracy of bombing attacks, and also demonstrated the lethal fanaticism of the Japanese pilots.

There was also disturbing news of barbarous treatment by the Japanese to Allied prisoners of war. All of these things were clearly portrayed in films, mostly American, which helped keep us in touch with Far East events, which were always overshadowed by our hazardous involvement in the European war.

It was with great relief that we learned that the battle

of the Atlantic had turned in our favour. U-boats were sunk in large numbers, and convoys got through without great losses.There was a time when shipping losses threatened supplies of food and war weapons, but mounting U-boat losses continued to allay such fears. Intensive bombing of Germany carried on apace, and large formations of bombers frequently passed over the town on their way to attack targets in France and Germany. It was reported that concentrated attacks had been made on railways and marshalling yards, which made us think that preparations were afoot for the long awaited second front.

There lingered misgivings over the heavy hilltop raid which had irritated some religious leaders who still questioned the morality of such a bombing raid. There had been considerable discussion and much soul searching on the subject, but it had been clearly pointed out by military experts that the hilltop advantage held by the German forces would have enabled then to inflict heavy casualties on Allied troops in their attempt to break through the German lines. That explanation surely should have cleared the air. However there were other things happening to hold our attention.

Large convoys of tanks and lorries regularly passed along our street, and although nobody knew where they were going, there was a general belief that an invasion across the Channel was not too far away, and as far as the gang was concerned there was chewing gum in plenty to collect as it was thrown from the military vehicles. At the next street corner meeting it was decided that a trip into the surrounding countryside was long overdue and one which would no doubt give us a better insight into what was actually taking place and gathering momentum. Mother, meanwhile, was showing a good deal of interest in a new radio personality called the 'Radio Doctor' He broadcast on a regular basis and, unfortunately, usually at breakfast time. This was not the time to be discussing constipation, stomach complaints and all manner of medical conditions. It was, of course, a valuable source of information and advice which clearly went some way to take the pressure of doctors and overburdened medical services, and in mother he certainly had a very interested listener. Our trip into the countryside offered us an amazing eye opener. Every wood and copse provided cover for tanks, lorries and other military equipment. Army camps had grown in size due to a huge number of additional tents to accommodate the ever growing number of military personnel. We thought that if this scene was repeated across a large part of the south, which rumours tended to confirm, then southern England would have resembled one large army camp. If there were any doubts that preparations for an invasion were taking place, these would have been swept away by the sight of invasion barges, which had been made in the railway works, being transported by road to the south coast or the nearest railhead. They were so huge that long diversions were needed to avoid some of the lower road bridges.

Rumours were rife, and what a wonderful forerunner of news they were as we learned that all manner of craft were being assembled along the whole length of the south coast. I couldn't help but wonder whether German agents and spies were keeping the Germans informed of all that was going on, for it was very clear that invasion would not come as a surprise. Maybe that hunch was right as heavy German guns across the channel began shelling Dover. That was yet another hazard that the poor people of Dover had to contend with, as the bombing and other actions off that part of the coast had given the area the name of 'Hellfire Corner'.

Although there was anticipation and excitement in the air, life carried on as normally as possible. The convoys continued to pass along our street, and the tank crews waved as they went by. On one occasion, it looked as though father had joined the column riding his bicycle, as he returned home from his allotment bearing peas, new potatoes, carrots and other home-grown things. Father's unscheduled appearance in the convoy gave the neighbours a good laugh, but we knew that he was always up for some fun if the opportunity arose.

We continued to live quite well considering the wartime circumstances. We were managing very well with the rationing, which I suppose was hardly surprising, seeing that we had dealt with the situation for several years, and father's home grown produce was also a boon, not only for us, but for the neighbours who had the benefit of produce which we found to be in excess of our needs.

There was long awaited relief for bombed out families, as temporary housing was constructed. The houses became known as prefabs, and consisted of two bedrooms, a living room and a kitchen. The prefabs must have been a blessing for the many homeless families who had been living with relatives, friends or making the most of rest centres and other makeshift accommodation.

We were approaching a period akin to many others where my geographical knowledge of place names was extremely enhanced. The Russians were making very good progress capturing many towns with strange sounding names to finally reach the Black Sea resort of Sevastopol.

There was also progress, although somewhat slower, as Allied forces pushed north through Italy, and finally took Monte Cassino, where the hilltop monastery fortress had been such a thorn in our side.

There were also rumours, by way of what we called the bush telegraph system, which was another way of saying from neighbour to neighbour, that a practice landing had been made in the West Country, but it was never confirmed as such information would have been useful to the Germans. Father, by way of working on the trains, was always in a position to hear news and rumours in plenty as he helped to transport service personnel.

The drive north in Italy continued, and it was a landmark in the Italian campaign when it was announced that Rome had been taken intact.

The Pope made it known that he was extremely thankful that the city, which he referred to as the eternal city, was unscathed, but German radio informed us that Hitler was the saviour of the city. Although this was clearly a propaganda exercise, I thought that it could possibly be true, not so much as a determined effort to save the city, but far more likely that Hitler's generals felt that to fall back would provide a more advantageous line of defence. This more thoughtful and planned approach was in complete contrast to Hitler's attitude in the early days of the war,when cities such as Warsaw and Rotterdam were raised to the ground if they were seen to be an unnecessary obstacle.

Whatever his attitude may have been, he must have felt very apprehensive about what lay ahead, as he could by now surely see that the war was definitely turning in our favour.

D-Day

It was a quiet morning, and we were having a leisurely breakfast of egg bacon and fried bread. Too much use of the frying pan was frowned upon by the health advisers and mother was once again listening to the Radio Doctor, who was so called because he had become well known by way of a regular breakfast slot on the BBC Home Service.

Our leisurely mood was suddenly interrupted by the sound of aircraft flying overhead, and judging by the increasing volume of noise they were passing over in large numbers. We were not too concerned, as we knew that the planes were unlikely to be German as they were severely stretched on other fronts, and there had been no enemy air activity for some considerable time. Nevertheless, as the sound continued to grow in intensity, we went into the garden to investigate, only to find that most neighbours had the same idea. Unfortunately, the cloud cover hid the aircraft from view, but this didn't stop Bert from next door informing us that something big was building, and it could be the start of the long awaited invasion. The retired major three doors down was somewhat sceptical. We were just about to retire indoors, when gaps began to appear in the cloud layer, and we could see aircraft towing gliders. All of the aircraft and gliders had white band markings around the wings and the fuselage. There was no doubting the general excitement, and Bert was convinced that the invasion had begun, and advised us all to listen to the next radio news bulletin. This we did and he was proved to be right. Landings had been made on the Normandy coast and the long awaited invasion, or second front, was well under way.

In the early days following the landings, news bulletins were eagerly awaited and listened to in silence. Sometimes when allied forces reached important objectives, radio programmes were interrupted and announcements made.

It was not all plain sailing though, and if anyone had thought that our forces would sweep quickly through France they were very much mistaken. The Germans had, over a long period of time, erected formidable obstacles on the beaches and built strong fortifications along the French coast, and fierce resistance made pushing inland from some of the beaches a very difficult and costly operation.

It was not until we saw the newsreel and press pictures of what seemed to be hundreds of naval vessels and a variety of other craft, that we realised what a huge seaborne invasion it had been. It was in fact later described as the greatest seaborne invasion in history.

It was little wonder that the second front was not rushed into as the agitators had wished, for it was clear that meticulous planning had been involved, and ingenuity of the highest order had been brought to bear.

It became abundantly clear to us laymen, that it was one thing to mount an invasion of thousands of troops across the Channel, but quite another to keep them supplied with arms, fuel and other vital supplies. To this end sections of a makeshift harbour were towed across the channel and erected on site along the French coast, and while this facility proved to be vital, it was no secret that the capture of large harbours such as Cherbourg was a pressing priority.

Reports of the fighting were relayed to us by reporters known as war correspondents, and were included in the news bulletins. One such reporter, whose descriptions of the action were clear and vivid, was Richard Dimbleby who, by way of his efficient and professional coverage, became a household name.

Although people were quite relieved that the invasion had been successfully carried out, there were some surprising mood changes on the home front. As far as the gang was concerned, the departure of American troops meant that the supply of chewing gum had dried up, but for some of the girls it was an entirely different matter. They had enjoyed a wonderful time with the troops who never appeared to be short of money and seemed to keep the girls supplied with nylon stockings, which was a must-have item at the time. It was the gang's comedian who wondered where American troops obtained nylon stockings as he could not see them being part of the kit issue.

Some girls had formed very close relationships with soldiers and were destined to become what were known as GI brides. They understandably felt low and concerned, knowing full well that some of the men folk would not return. It was unfortunate that race became an issue as some people did not look too kindly on those who had made relationships with black soldiers but, ironically, condemned the system of segregation between black and white operated by the American authorities.

Other changes became noticeable due to the departure of military personnel. The dance halls were somewhat quieter. Although the American import of jitterbugging continued, the occasional clashes between the British and American troops looked to be a thing of the past. That is not to say that the military presence had entirely disappeared, for there was a constant movement of troops and vehicles through the town, but mostly they were en route to reinforce the fighting divisions in France.

A Secret Weapon

Hitler had at times made mention of a secret weapon, which he said would bring this country to its knees. We treated this with indifference, and once the Normandy invasion was under way we had more important things on which to focus our attention. That was until one day in early June.

News broke of very fast-flying objects crossing the south coast and flying towards London. On reaching London, an automatic device shut down the engine and the craft plummeted to the ground where there was a huge explosion causing heavy damage over a wide area. It was ascertained that the nose of the aircraft was a warhead which contained around one ton of explosive

Consequently Londoners, who had enjoyed freedom from air raids since the days of the blitz now faced another terror. The craft was propelled by a very powerful engine which enabled it to reach a speed of around four hundred miles an hour, and sounded to me like a very large motor bike. It eventually became known as the Doodlebug.

It was discovered that the flying bombs took off from launching ramps at many sites in Northern France, and so it was vital that Allied forces advanced quickly across France in order to capture and destroy the weapons and launching sites.

The RAF carried out raids on the launching sites in an

effort to stem the tide as the number of doodlebugs crossing the coast increased daily. The task was made more difficult as the Germans also operated from mobile launching sites.

As it was, London came under constant bombardment, and the city was once again sustaining heavy damage

It was proving difficult to defend against such speedy aircraft, which travelled faster than the Spitfires that had proved so wonderfully effective in the Battle of Britain. The Spitfire did in fact have some degree of success, and shot down quite a few. Bert next door was well up with the situation as usual, and had heard that our pilots had tried to fly along side the craft and tip them off-course with their wings.

Our town was not in the firing line at that time, nor was most of southern England, and we were hopeful of a speedy advance across France to nullify the doodlebug threat. Unfortunately the drive towards the town of Caen and the port of Cherbourg was held up by a stubborn German resistance. There was better news on the Russian front where the Russians had begun a huge offensive and made strident advances.

For us kids it was a time to take stock. We had over a period of four wartime years generally kept in touch with all the military action that was taking place, even being aware of military leaders from both sides, The names of Montgomery, Eisenhower, Rommel, and many more were no strangers to us. However, at that particular time probably more than any other, one became aware that the war was indeed a world war. It was being fought on so many fronts. The second front, the Russian front, the push northwards in Italy together with the war in the Far East where our troops were fighting in Burma and American forces were overrunning the Japanese as they captured islands in the Pacific. A clear head was needed when listening to the wireless at news times, when bulletins constantly updated situations in all of the war zones. Also it was becoming clear that, barring a disastrous change in fortune, an allied victory was likely in the not too distant future, and we began to wonder what the future had in store. It was also a time to acknowledge that we had matured significantly from the young tearaway rebels that we were at the start of the war.

The gang's street corner meetings still took place, but were slightly more sober affairs which no doubt reflected our growing maturity. There was also the small matter of the looming final school year ending with the examinations for school certificate.

I suddenly became aware of the importance of achieving the school certificate, for I thought that it would determine the kind of job that I would do, and the type of work that I would undertake. My mind went back to the days when well-meaning ladies would ask 'And what would you like to be?' I think that an engine driver was a common reply to that question, but as for me I really had no idea. What concerned me more was that time had moved on and I still had no idea. Perhaps this was because there were other things on which to concentrate our minds during the more hazardous times of the war. However, this was not something that could be put to the back of my mind.

One member of the family who had no such worries was the cat. What a lovely care-free life he had led during the war years. Even during the most stressful times, when he seemed unaware of falling bombs and gunfire, he just curled up in his corner of the table shelter and enjoyed the moment.

Perhaps it was a time for us as a family to be thankful, for we had thus far come through unscathed and with a home intact and undamaged, unlike thousands of people who had been bombed out and lived with friends or in other temporary accommodation. It was abundantly clear that a huge house building programme was needed as quickly as possible, and announcements were made, regarding such projects, not only for the building of houses but also for social and welfare schemes.

I suppose that planning in advance was at the time the right and proper option, but I couldn't help feeling, unlike some people, that the war was far from over, and that many twists and turns in fortunes lay ahead, But it seemed that, come what may, our set routines carried on as usual. June and her mother still went to the pictures on a Monday, something that they had been doing throughout the war. We still took our Sunday summer evening walks after church, although there was a surprising additional venue to visit over and above father's allotment garden and the town gardens.

The town's football ground and cricket grounds were close together, and both had been taken over to house prisoners of war. The Germans were allocated to the football ground, which had the potential to be more secure, while the Italians appeared to be allowed to roam around the cricket ground with seemingly little supervision. The gang's comedian didn't miss the chance to remind us that the Italians were better lovers than fighters. This was borne out by the fact that quite a few of the prisoners were seen with some of the local girls, a situation that the girls apparently found acceptable, seeing that the Italians had ceased hostilities, leaving the Germans to fight on all fronts.

The girls obviously found the venue an attraction, but also many people chose to get a close up view of those who were former enemies.

The gang was more interested in going to the pictures to see the comedy capers of Will Hay, and Laurel and Hardy. Even while at the cinema we were kept informed of breaking news. A home-made slide, which had been hastily put together by the cinema projectionist, was projected on to the screen to inform the audience of any significant developments or achievements.

It was clear that much in the way of supplies for our forces was still on the way, as many military vehicles and equipment continued to come down our street and pass our house.

Caen was at last taken after a month's strong opposition, and we hoped that it would be the start of a swift advance across France to overrun the launching sites from where the doodlebugs had brought havoc to London.

As the attack on London continued it prompted mother to ask my aunt if she would like to come down and stay with us for a while, as she did during the days of the blitz, but on this occasion she opted to stay put and weather the storm. She said that there had been talk of another evacuation of children, due to the constant danger, but not on the same scale as the evacuation in 1939.

News was beginning to come through regarding atrocities carried out against the Jews. They were said to be transported to camps in the occupied countries and then gassed. Bert, as always was first to hear about this, and although no one openly doubted the authenticity of his reports, this particular piece of news was much too horrendous to contemplate.

A much better piece of news was the announcement of a Glen Miller tour with his orchestra. There was no better time for such a tour for he had made countless fans who had enjoyed his music. They had also played for the Jitterbug dance and other robust routines regularly seen in the dance halls.

There was no doubting the impact that the American presence had on the lives of those who came into contact with them. They had broken down the barriers of the good old British reserve, some had established relationships with local girls, and others had made friends with quite a few families.

Liberation Begins

The first continental capital to be liberated was Paris and pictures of the tremendous event were a joy to see. Crowds waving flags lined the streets to greet the Allied troops, Many experienced the joy of being kissed while others were showered with flowers. Paris had suffered under the, German occupation, and one could only imagine the great feeling of relief that was obviously felt by the Parisians. The liberation of Paris was followed by the liberation of Marseilles following the successful landing on the southern French coast. The French women who were known to have collaborated with the Germans suffered the indignity of having their heads shaved, so that all could see who the collaborators were.

The race across France to Belgium continued apace and the people of Brussels were the next to experience the joy of liberation. One wondered what was going through Hitler's mind, as not only were the Germans retreating in the west, but the Russians were sweeping through the Balkans. The gang's comedian would have summed it up neatly but he had returned to London following the V1 menace which had virtually come to an end. He had returned with mixed feelings after having established himself as one of the gang's leaders to enjoy immensely his stay with us. His departure coincided with the arrival of the gang's new found maturity. For the last five years we had lived and often laughed our way through the wartime years and we were aware how quickly we had grown up, or perhaps it would be more accurate to say how circumstances determined how quickly we had grown up. Perhaps the term gang was no longer a right and proper description of us.

Allied troops were sweeping across northern France and there appeared little to stop them reaching the German frontier. Bert reckoned that the war would be over by Christmas, and he was not alone in thinking that. The vicar announced that a service of thanksgiving would be held as soon as peace had been declared. This news was gratefully received by many parishioners who were of the opinion that the end of the war was in sight. My own view was that such thoughts were a little premature to say the least, especially as the Germans still seemed capable of giving us unpleasant surprises as was the case with the VI buzz bombs.

My pessimistic view was vindicated when suddenly news broke of a new terror, although it was some time before we were given the full facts. It appeared that several large explosions had occurred in the London area, which we were told had been caused by escaping gas. My aunt in London said that when the events occurred, people spoke of an explosion followed by a peculiar rushing sound similar to an express train quickly passing. It was later admitted by government ministers that no announcement had been made in order not to alarm the public, but the stark reality of the situation was the arrival of a number of rockets with explosive warheads which was the German V2 weapon. Against this there was absolutely no defence, as it was launched from German or occupied territory and travelled upwards eventually arcing towards its target in the London area. For Londoners there was no warning of impending disaster, but some spoke of being able to see the reflected sunlight on the rocket as it descended towards its target.

There was considerable damage and many casualties caused by this horrendous weapon as London again bore the brunt of enemy attacks, and it was imperative that the sweep of Allied troops towards Germany to overrun the rocket launching sites was carried out as quickly as possible, although of course, that was easier said than done.

The official and final indication that attacks on this country were a thing of the past, was the decision to stand down the Home Guard which was made up of men who, for one reason or another, were unable to serve in the armed forces, or who were too old to do so.

Although the decision to stand down the Home Guard was a good sign regarding the war situation, I felt that the move resulted in mixed feelings among some members, who had not only carried out their duties with gusto, but had also enjoyed the camaraderie. It was this which had proved to be an important part of the exercise.

While there was a mood of optimism following the relaxation of wartime restrictions, it must be remembered that the V2 rockets were still falling on London and this made us realise that the timing of the invasion had been important, for had the landings been delayed further, the Germans would have been able to launch many more VI and V2 weapons unhindered, which would have resulted in further destruction of London and other areas in southern England Moreover, it may even have altered the course of the war. However, I had not too much time to dwell on that possible outcome for exams were looming and there was homework and revision to be done. This was all the more vexing as there were new films to be seen in the run-up to Christmas. Previous years had always seen many good films released at that time and this year was no exception. The emphasis appeared to he on dramatic offerings The brilliant Laurence Olivier played 'Richard The Third' and the well loved John Gielgud received tremendous acclaim for his performance in 'Hamlet'. The cinema had enjoyed great support during the war years and was still enjoying good houses. Audiences for concerts of classical music had also remained high, and the Henry Wood promenade concerts had come round again, although sadly Sir Henry Wood had died earlier in the year and was unable to celebrate the fiftieth anniversary of the concerts. I had, over the years, grown to love the sound of a large symphony orchestra, and the music of the great composers, and this was in no small measure due to the encouragement given by our teachers, particularly our music mistress who brought her portable gramophone into the classroom, and played for us what she described as the music of the masters. There were also times when we attended the school's afternoon orchestral performances and I came to enjoy them, in spite of the fact that the main object in attending was to miss the afternoon lessons.

In the field of dance music American band leader Glen Miller had proved to be extremely popular and had given us many memorable tunes, but there was considerable concern when his flight to Paris where he was scheduled to give a concert was reported to be overdue.

The results of the Christmas exams showed that I had improved somewhat on past performances which was just as well as the school certificate exams were just around the corner. The same could not be said of dancing at the school soirée. This was in spite of efforts by our woodwork teacher who quite remarkably ended the woodwork lesson early in order to teach us how to dance the waltz. On the night of the dance I made every effort to steer clear of him on the dance floor so that he would be unable to see clearly that his instruction had been a complete waste of time.

It was hoped that the approaching Christmas would be

the last in wartime although it had to be remembered that Londoners were still under threat from the V2 rockets, and it was this that prompted mother to ensure that my aunt would be with us tor the festive period.

It always amazed me how mother provided such a good table, even in spite of the rationing and shortages. Father's turn of duty ensured that he would be home for Christmas dinner but was required to book on in the afternoon for a two to ten shift. All that remained now was the announcement which always heralded the arrival of the home-made wine that mother had produced. This she had made consistently throughout the war years in an effort to augment the port and sherry which we always enjoyed at Christmas.

There was however, breaking news which threatened to dampen the festive spirit. The Germans had broken through the Allied lines in France, and had made substantial advances, particularly in the north of the region. An examination of the map showed that a successful push north by the German forces would not only provide an incentive to retake the port of Antwerp but could also surround large numbers of British troops in Belgium and Holland. It was noticeable that Bert next door had remained quiet since he assured us that the war would be over by Christmas and it was the Major who lived a few doors down who was holding court over the garden wall. As if to lift spirits at the time, large numbers of American bombers flew over the town on the way to targets in Germany and made a very spectacular sight as well as providing a major confidence boost

Christmas was enjoyed by all and New Year's Eve had come round once again. Surely this would be the last wartime New Year's Eve. The early signs were encouraging. The Russians had launched a major offensive in Poland, and soon afterwards Warsaw, the first capital city to be occupied by the Germans, fell to he Russians after five years of occupation. The offensive was led by Marshal Zhukov, a name which was new to the gang, and one which was duly noted. A speedy advance across Poland followed, and Russian troops freed a concentration camp at Auschwitz. Clearly, the Germans had had no time to clear and evacuate what had been known as a death camp, and pictures in the press and cinema newsreels revealed the horrendous conditions endured by the prisoners. People wandered around, with vacant faces, seemingly oblivious to what was going on around them. Some prisoners resembling living skeletons ambled around aimlessly. Piles of spectacles, clothing and all manner or human paraphernalia could be seen, and one could hardly contemplate the nightmare existence they had endured over many months or years.

We had heard of the existence or such camps, and of efforts to systematically eliminate the Jews, and here we saw the terrifying pictures which provided the proof. It was gratifying to hear, soon after, that the Red Army had advanced to a position one hundred miles from Berlin. On the western side, the allies had fought furiously to repel the breakthrough in France, which had threatened to seriously disrupt the Allied push toward the German frontier, Fortunately, after a bitter struggle the tide turned in favour of the Allied forces and the push began once again towards the Siegfried line. During the exciting advance towards the German frontier cinema audiences were constantly kept informed of progress by hastily made slides which were projected on to the screen Such was the case during one of the gang's visits, or should I now say one of the group's visits to the cinema, when we were informed that Allied forces had reached the Siegfried line, news which was greeted with an enormous cheer. It had been five years since we had sung a song about the Siegfried line together with other songs which denigrated the German leaders. I wonder if I can recall it now:

We're going to hang out the washing on the Siegfried line
Have you any dirty washing mother dear
We're going to hang out the washing on the Siegfried line
If the Siegfried line's still there
Whether the weather may be wet or fine
We will wash away without a care
We're going to hang out the washing on the Siegfried line
If the Siegfried line's still there

The aircraft towing gliders which made a spectacular sight on D-day were in the air again. and it was reported that paratroops had been dropped in the area of Arnhem. The object of the exercise was a subject for the over the garden wall discussion in which Bert was always prominent, but in this discussion he seemed to play second fiddle to the retired Major. Tragically, the reality of the situation was grim. In what seemed little over a week, British troops were forced to withdraw from the area, having sustained heavy losses, and the operation which had apparently been mounted in a tactical bid to shorten the war was deemed to be a costly failure. There was even more cause for regret as the V2 rocket attacks on London, which had somewhat subsided, began once again, launched from sites in the Netherlands. My aunt told us that the rockets had caused considerable damage and many casualties.

Taking into account the failure of the operation at Arnhem and the rocket attacks on London, there was a feeling that although our forces had reached Aachen, the German resistance was stiffening and it was clear that the war was far from over.

V E Day

Attention was suddenly diverted from wartime action when the sudden death of American President Roosevelt was announced. There were those who had criticised him, as they believed that he should have entered America into the war much sooner. However, he had over the passage of time proved to be a staunch ally.

The speedy advance across Germany continued as troops pressed towards Bremen and Hamburg. I wondered what was going through the mind of Hitler as he cowered in Berlin, contemplating Russian forces closing in from the east, and allied forces advancing from the west. The position in which he found himself was seen as the setting of a just and proper end to a tyrant who had brought so much terror and grief to the people of the occupied countries. None more so than the appalling atrocities carried out in the many concentration camps.

The awful evidence of this was seen when allied troops freed the concentration camp at Buchenwald. We had already seen the pictures of the Auschwitz camp horrors, but the scenes at Buchenwald were simply unbelievable. Figures resembling walking skeletons wandered around with expressions of despair apparently unable to comprehend their moment of release from cruelty and degradation. There was a huge open grave which contained hundreds of naked bodies. Lines of ovens where bodies had been burned were surrounded by piles of clothing and other personal items. People in the cinema watching the newsreel sat in stunned silence as the camera filmed a party being guided around the area with looks of horrific disbelief, some holding handkerchiefs to their noses as they tried to avoid bodies which had not been thrown into the open grave. We had often heard rumours of such atrocities, but those who witnessed the horrific reality will have retained those memories to the present day.

Exciting news broke that Russian forces had encircled Berlin, which prompted many people to think that the end of the war was just around the corner. It prompted the parish vicar to announce that the thanksgiving service would be held on the day that the end of hostilities was announced. The fall of the Reichstag caused great excitement but no one seemed to know what had happened to Hitler. Even Bert, who had been quite successful with his wartime predictions, was unable to come up with an answer, although he said that the best thing that Hitler could do would be to commit suicide. His wife Gladys, whose infectious laughter had kept our spirits up during the most testing times, seemed for once to be quite subdued. It was clear that such a momentous occasion, marking the end of the war after five years of bitter struggle, would be received, not only with joy and laughter, but also with moments of sadness and regret, remembering those who had lost their lives.

The actual surrender took place in Germany at the location of Lüneburg Heath. General Montgomery, who had led many successful operations during the war, presided over the proceedings. Newsreel and press pictures showed him proudly enjoying the moment as he watched one German commander after another sign the official documents.

We all then eagerly awaited the official announcement that hostilities had come to an end which eventually came at around three o'clock on a day in May and was made by Winston Churchill.

The thanksgiving service which was held later and which we attended as a family was attended by a large congregation. The church was situated in the town centre and, as we left following the service, we found ourselves right in the midst of boisterous celebration. Crowds of people were gathered in the surrounding area dancing and singing with the more energetic climbing lamp posts and performing other gymnastic feats. The rather rude lyrics to some of the songs being sung caused mother to usher us by quite quickly. Newsreel and press pictures of the celebrations soon followed which showed the King and Queen on the balcony of Buckingham Palace acknowledging the vast crowds below.

Victory celebrations continued apace. The pubs did a roaring trade and flags began to appear everywhere. Apart from the flags flying on public buildings, residents displayed flags from their front windows, and in narrow residential streets small flags were strung from one side of the street to the other, which made a splendid sight and a perfect backdrop to the street parties that followed. The ladies hastily formed a committee to organise and preside over the street celebrations. Much had to be done. Trestle tables had to be obtained, and as our party was held in a side street off the main road, the tables were able to be erected in the middle of the road. Rationing was still in being, but appeared not to adversely affect proceedings. An extremely good selection of sandwiches, cakes, fruit, jelly, trifles and a variety of drinks were enjoyed by all. Many people supplied crockery and glasses for the occasion, and most of those partaking of the feast brought with them their own chairs.

The ladies of the committee took on the task of pouring the drinks and overseeing the proceedings, and wore paper aprons which they had made of colours red white and blue.

The party scene made a very splendid and patriotic sight. Following the tea and later in the evening, there was dancing in the street. Perhaps the music provided by the small group may not have been of the highest of standard, but who cared, it was an occasion to be enjoyed, and enjoy it we did. Some young men who, after having quite a few drinks, decided to cause some humour by dressing as ladies and made their appearance looking well groomed and carrying the obligatory handbags, which caused much amusement. I don't think that the term 'men in drag' was used in those days, but if it was I had never heard of it. Not all parties were held on the same day, and quite a few people joined in the fun and games at parties in the surrounding streets

There were numerous civic occasions, and a huge VE sign ('Victory in Europe') was erected on the clock tower of the town hall building, and made a good centrepiece when it was illuminated at night.

Many events celebrating victory were held such as dances and parades, and even the more subdued occasions such as the seemingly popular whist drives were frequently advertised.

On reflection, as pupils, we thought that we had done well during those exciting times by refraining from being completely distracted from studies and, quite remarkably, at least as far as I was concerned, achieved far better exam results than I had done for some considerable time.

After the celebrations had died down, it was time for the nation to look to the future and set about tackling the many problems that lay ahead.

As a result of the heavy raids on British cities, thousands of houses had been destroyed or damaged, and a huge house- building programme had to be undertaken. A start had already been made with the building of temporary accommodation which we called 'prefabs' and seemed to be of a reasonably good standard.

Some of the men who had been serving in the armed forces for a period of a few years would probably need a new wardrobe, or at least a new suit. The problem was overcome by the issue of a new suit to those being demobbed, and not unnaturally these became known as demob suits. While they looked to be of a fairly good standard, I don't think that the wearer expected to look an example of sartorial elegance.

There were also problems of a human nature. Some men returned home to find that their wives had been unfaithful, and in some cases had entered into a relationship with someone else. The war years had seen a deterioration of moral standards and behaviour, which was seen as one of the most unfortunate outcomes.

On a more positive note, quite a few girls were starting out on a new adventure, as they were about to marry, or had already married American servicemen, and looked forward to starting a new life in the United States. They became known as GI brides.

After the victory celebrations had subsided and we looked to the future, there was no disguising the fact that the political situation looked uncertain both at home and in Europe. At home there was a need to hold a general election following the end of a wartime coalition government, and so far as Europe was concerned it should be remembered that although Britain and Russia fought together against the common enemy, Russia or the Soviet Union as it was then called, was a communist state, which did not sit well with British democracy.

Moreover, Bert, who had been unusually quite, had clearly discussed the situation, with the major and confidently predicted that as Russian troops had been the first to enter Berlin, the capital German city, quite a few problems would lay ahead.

He proved to be right, for, in the event, Russians occupied East Germany, and the British and Americans occupied western Germany, but Berlin was divided into four sectors, which was not looked upon at home as a satisfactory situation. There was continued speculation over what had happened to Hitler. There were rumours that he had committed suicide and his body burned in close proximity to the bunker, where he had spent his last desperate days.

There was no such speculation regarding Lord Haw Haw, the traitor William Joyce who had given us so much amusement.. He was sent for trial for High Treason. About two months after the victory celebrations, the anticipated general election was held. I wondered what Winston Churchill's thoughts were as after having led Britain brilliantly through the war, he had to endure the formation of a Labour government.

The nation had decided that a Labour government was best to tackle the social problems, and there were of course many problems relating to housing, employment, health and, not least, there were financial problems following years of financing the war effort.

Churchill had however warned that although victory in Europe merited a worthy celebration, ruthless Japan had still to be overcome. Indeed many British troops were fighting in Burma and in other surrounding locations and so, after a brief respite, our attention had to be focused on the hostilities in the Far East.

Time to Adjust

There was a spring in our step as we looked forward to a good summer. The exams had come and gone and the eight weeks school holidays were ahead. The final school assembly prior to the summer holidays was always quite a fine occasion, and we always sang a song which I thought was more in keeping with a higher college or university.

Forty years on when afar and asunder
Parted are those who are singing today
When you look back and forgetfully wonder
What you were like in your work and your play
Then it will be there will often come o'er you
Glimpses of life and the sound of a song
Feeble of foot and rheumatic of shoulder
What will it be for you forty years on.

It was a stirring song which conveyed the academic spirit of the occasion.

We were about to enjoy our last summer holiday before our final term, and I detected a shift in attitude towards us from the staff. Perhaps they gave us a little more respect as we were now more mature students about to embark on our final year in the fifth form, which would end with the examination for school certificate and matriculation.

There was however the summer to enjoy and families

made the most of it, certainly our family did. Trips were made to the seaside, and those who lived near the south coast resorts were able to access beaches which had been cleared of barbed wire and all manner of obstacles which had been erected to deter enemy landings.

It was clear to see, when passing through towns and cities, that great strides had been made clearing and tidying the bombed sites as local authorities looked to the future. Our household had not kept pace with the momentum though, and I noticed that the blackout screens which father had made still remained in our garden shed awaiting disposal.

On the downside, rationing was of course still with us, and we were informed that it would be with us for some considerable time. The war in the Far East seemed very distant, which was not very surprising following the European wartime situation where everyone was in the front line. American films graphically portrayed the struggle as American forces invaded and took Pacific islands en route to Japan.

Obviously that was all well and good, but the overriding thought, which came into our minds over and over again, was how on earth could a seaborne invasion be mounted against the large island of Japan.

British forces were fighting in Burma and other theatres of war in the Far East, and the war did not seem so distant when we heard of those we knew who were involved in the fighting.

There was more excitement on the home front as yet more girls were excitedly preparing to depart for America to become GI brides. I wondered how many would stay, and how many would return, for all that they knew of life in the United States was what they had been told and what they had seen in American films.

These must have been difficult times for the families

involved, and I wondered how our family would have felt had my sister been one of those leaving the country to start a new life.

As it was, I noticed very little change in our family routines and attitude. We still practised good manners, and father always raised his hat when meeting the ladies. Most men still stood up when ladies entered the room, and so it appeared that, although the war had changed, many ways, lifestyles, and good manners were still the order of the day.

Horrific Destruction

Although good manners may well have prevailed, I had the feeling that life would never be quite the same again. For example there had been a relaxation of the strict moral standards to which we had become accustomed, and some girls had become pregnant who were not married which caused a few whispered conversations.

Such things did not interest the more mature group who played football during the summer months as not enough lads seemed to be interested in cricket. The park where we played still retained a rather uneven surface as a result of the bomb craters which had been filled in, but that did not deter us from enjoying a rather primitive kickabout making use of a couple of coats to mark where the goal posts should be.

The war in the Far East came sharply into focus, as we heard of heavy raids on Tokyo and other important Japanese cities. There was a feeling among some military leaders that heavy blows delivered by concentrated air power would lead to a fairly quick surrender. This proved to be wishful thinking as the Japanese leaders were quick to reject an unconditional surrender. We were then resigned to the fact that the war with Japan would appear to be endless, having regard to the seemingly impossible task of mounting a seaborne invasion.

We were, of course, completely unaware of the forthcoming

events which marked a momentous occasion in history and brought the war with Japan to a sudden end.

The news broke of an air raid on Japan. It was not a conventional air raid made by a large number of bombers, but a raid which was made by just one single bomber armed with one particularly destructive weapon.

The weapon was an atomic bomb, and was dropped on the city of Hiroshima. The explosion brought about scenes of destruction, the scale of which had never been seen before. Newsreel pictures showed an awesome gigantic cloud which rose to the height of many thousands of feet. Countless victims were killed, maimed or eliminated by the blast and radiation, and the centre of the city was raised to the ground.

It goes without saying that there were grave misgivings in some quarters regarding the morality of such destruction inflicted on a civilian population. I found, as did many others, that the only way to arrive at anywhere near an appropriate attitude, was to accept that the action was the lesser of two evils. There was also the need to consider how many more thousands of lives would have been lost had the struggle continued. There was the 'eye for an eye' attitude, considering the atrocities carried out on prisoners forced to work under appalling conditions building bridges and rail roads.

Whatever the thoughts at the time, there was no immediate Japanese surrender. A few days later a second atom bomb was dropped on the city of Nagasaki. Ultimately faced by the possible continuation of such destruction, the Japanese leaders surrendered unconditionally. What had seemed like the prospect of a very long drawn out conflict, was brought to a sudden end by the use of terrifying weapons dropped from the air.

The celebrations on VJ day, as it was known, were not on

the scale of those marking the end of the war in Europe but, nevertheless, parties were held, and there was tremendous relief that hostilities worldwide had at last come to an end.

There was then the task of facing up to the problems of peace, and they were considerable. A large house-building programme was needed to accommodate the many families whose homes had been destroyed as a result of the blitz. Returning members of the armed forces would need jobs following their demobilisation, with many hoping to work in factories where production had returned to a normal manufacturing base following the production of the weapons of war.

The gigantic task of rebuilding our war-torn cities would surely take many years. For me, the final exams for the school certificate had to be faced, and it was with great relief that I came through successfully.

Obviously the gang broke up and went their ways as a new working life beckoned. Some stayed in town while others looked for pastures new.

We had grown up from children to young men during those war years, and no one has since, or will ever again live through such times.

Did the experience have any undesirable effect upon me? I honestly believe that the effect was quite the opposite. I learned to cope with stress and tragedy and to abide by a strict discipline, both in the school environment, and in adhering to the wartime restrictions, things which have held me in good stead over the many years which have passed.